brownies & bars

brownies & bars

Liz Franklin

photography by Tara Fisher

You know you deserve a treat. Take a break, put your feet up and bite into **something sweet 6**. Surely everyone's favourite flavours – chocolate and coffee. Just perfect when you fancy **something sticky 34**. Raspberries, apples, plums, bananas and oranges – add a delicious twist to your baking by stirring in **something fruity 52**. Naughty but nice, impossible to resist, tempt your friends with **something special 70**. Can't find that recipe? Check the **index 94**.

Something Sweet

Baklava

Makes 16
Preparation time: 1 hour, plus soaking
You will need a lightly buttered roasting tin or cake
tin measuring 18 x 30 cm/7 x 12 inches

300 g/10 oz pistachio nuts, or mixed walnuts and
pistachios, roughly chopped
50 g/1¾ oz ground almonds
2 teaspoons ground cinnamon
200 g/7 oz filo pastry
150 g/5 oz butter, melted
juice and zest 2 large oranges
juice 1 lemon
200 ml/7 fl oz water
200 g/7 oz caster sugar

For anyone who has a sweet tooth and a passion for nuts, these syrupy little pastries are absolute nirvana. They're equally as good with a cup (or two) of strong mid morning coffee as they are the final flourish to a Middle Eastern inspired supper. Until the notion of reverse calories has been patented and perfected, please don't give a moment's thought to such things; just tuck in and enjoy – and simply power walk to work in the morning.

Preheat the oven to 180°C/350°F/gas mark 4. Mix the pistachios, ground almonds and cinnamon together and set aside.

Layer half of the filo pastry in the tin, brushing each sheet generously with melted butter as you go. Scatter the nuts evenly over the pastry. Cover with the remaining filo pastry, again brushing generously with melted butter between each sheet. Brush the top generously with more melted butter. Tuck the edge of the pastry in and carefully cut a diamond pattern through the whole baklava.

Bake for 20 minutes and then turn down the oven temperature to 150°C/300°F/gas mark 2 and bake for a further 10 minutes or so, until crisp and golden.

Meanwhile, heat the orange juice and zest, lemon juice, water and sugar in a saucepan until the sugar has melted. Bubble for 4–5 minutes, until the syrup has thickened, and then leave to cool.

Remove the baklava from the oven and pour over the syrup. Leave for several hours to allow the syrup to soak into the pastry, and then store in an airtight container.

Iced Passion Fruit Squares

Makes 15
Preparation time: 1¼ hours, plus cooling
You will need a lightly buttered deep roasting tin or cake tin measuring 20 x 30 cm/8 x 12 inches

250 g/9 oz butter
250 g/9 oz caster sugar
4 eggs, beaten
250 g/9 oz self-raising flour
juice and zest 2 oranges

Icing
5 juicy passion fruit, halved
400 g/14 oz icing sugar
50 g/1¾ oz butter, softened

Preheat the oven to 180°C/350°F/gas mark 4. Cream the butter and sugar together until pale and fluffy and then beat in the eggs, a little at a time until the mixture is smooth. You may have to add a little flour in between each addition to prevent the mixture curdling. Stir in the remaining flour, the orange juice and zest.

Spoon into the prepared tin and bake for 50 minutes, or until risen and golden. Cool in the tin.

Once the cake is cold, scoop the pulp from four of the passion fruit into a sieve and press the juice through the sieve into a bowl. Discard the seeds. Beat the passion fruit juice into the icing sugar with the softened butter. Spread over the cake. Drizzle over the pulp and seeds of the remaining passion fruit, leave to set and then cut into squares. Store in an airtight container.

No Nut Brownies

Makes 15
Preparation time: 55 minutes
You will need a lightly buttered roasting tin or cake tin measuring 20 x 25 cm/8 x 10 inches

250 g/9 oz butter
500 g/1 lb 2 oz caster sugar
100 g/3½ oz cocoa powder
4 eggs, beaten
100 g/3½ oz self-raising flour

If you have a tub of good quality cocoa powder in the cupboard (and for this I do mean real unsweetened cocoa rather than sweet drinking chocolate) and fresh eggs to hand, then these dense and delicious brownies can be rustled up in next to no time. And despite being nut-free, they're still very special. Cut into little bite-size squares they make handsome petits fours. Take care not to overcook them, however, as the texture should be squidgy not spongy.

Preheat the oven to 180°C/350°F/gas mark 4. Melt the butter, sugar and cocoa powder together in a saucepan over a gentle heat. Remove the pan from the heat, cool slightly and stir in the eggs. Fold in the flour.

Spoon the mixture into the prepared tin and bake for 35 minutes or so, until just firm but still fudgy.

Allow to cool in the tin and then cut into squares. Store in an airtight container.

Date and Walnut Squares

Makes 15
Preparation time: 1¼ hours
You will need a lightly buttered deep roasting tin
or cake tin measuring 20 x 30 cm/8 x 12 inches

250 g/9 oz butter
250 g/9 oz golden caster sugar
4 eggs, beaten
250 g/9 oz self-raising flour, sifted
100 g/3½ oz dates, pitted and chopped
100 g/3½ oz walnuts, roughly chopped
150 ml/5 fl oz maple syrup

These squares often take pole position in the sweet
section of any picnic box I have a hand in preparing.
Sticky dates and crunchy walnuts hovering in feathery
light sponge do make a great combo, and a quick slick
of maple syrup over the cooled cake adds another
quite irresistible dimension. Only the real McCoy will
do though – the sticky, concentrated sap of the maple
tree. No sickly sweet impostors masquerading as
'maple flavoured syrup'.

Preheat the oven to 180°C/350°F/gas mark 4. Cream the
butter and sugar together until pale and fluffy and then beat
in the eggs, a little at a time, until the mixture is smooth.
Add a little flour in between each addition to stop the
mixture curdling. Stir in the remaining flour, the dates and
walnuts. Spoon the mixture into the prepared tin. Bake for
30 minutes or so, until risen and golden.

Allow to cool in the tin. Once the cake is cold, brush it
with the maple syrup and cut it into squares. Store in an
airtight container.

Coconut Slice

Makes 15
Preparation time: 1 hour, plus 30 minutes
resting for the pastry
You will need a Swiss roll tin measuring
23 x 30 cm/9 x 12 inches

Pastry
175 g/6 oz butter
50 g/1¾ oz caster sugar
1 egg yolk
320 g/11 oz plain flour, sifted
450 g/1 lb raspberry jam

Topping
500 g/1 lb 2oz coconut
300 g/10 oz caster sugar
4 eggs, beaten
100 g/3½ oz butter, melted

To make the pastry, cream the butter and sugar together
until light and smooth and then beat in the egg yolk. Add
the flour, and bring the mixture together to form a smooth
pastry dough. Wrap the pastry in plastic wrap and chill in
the fridge for 30 minutes.

Preheat the oven to 180°C/350°F/gas mark 4. Roll the
pastry out to cover the base of the tin and trim the edges
neatly. Spread the jam evenly over the pastry.

To make the topping, mix the coconut, sugar and eggs
together. Stir in the butter. Spread the mixture evenly over
the jam. Bake for 25–30 minutes, until golden and firm.
Allow to cool in the tin and then cut into slices. Store in
an airtight container.

Linzertorte Slices

Makes 25
Preparation time: 1 hour and 10 minutes, plus
30 minutes resting for the pastry
You will need a Swiss roll tin measuring 24 x 36 cm/
9½ x 14 inches

375 g/13 oz butter
375 g/13 oz sugar
3 egg yolks, beaten
375 g/13 oz plain flour
100 g/3½ oz ground almonds
750 g/1½ lb raspberry jam
caster sugar, for sprinkling

Cream the butter and sugar together in a large bowl until
light and fluffy. Add the eggs, a little at a time, and beat until
they are all full incorporated. Stir in the flour and ground
almonds and bring the mixture together to form a smooth,
soft pastry dough. Wrap in plastic wrap and chill in the
fridge for 30 minutes to firm up.

Preheat the oven to 180°C/350°F/gas mark 4. Lightly
flour a work surface then roll out slightly less than half the
pastry and use it to line the baking tin. Spread the jam in
an even layer over the pastry.

Roll out the remaining pastry and cut it into long strips
about 1cm/½ inch wide. Use the strips to form a lattice
pattern over the jam. Bake for 25–30 minutes, or until
golden brown. Remove from the oven and leave to cool.

Sprinkle a little caster sugar over the linzertorte and cut
into slices or bars. Store in an airtight container.

Rosemary and Raisin Squares

Makes 15
Preparation time: 1 hour and 10 minutes
You will need a lightly buttered deep roasting tin
or cake tin measuring 20 x 30 cm/8 x 12 inches

250 g/9 oz butter
250 g/9 oz caster sugar
4 eggs, beaten
250 g/9 oz self-raising flour
1 tbsp finely chopped fresh rosemary
150 g/5 oz raisins
2 tablespoons caster sugar, for sprinkling

These squares are simply divine. The idea for cubes of
cake speckled with fresh rosemary and plump raisins
came from my son Oli's passion for the rosemary and
raisin bread sold at my local Italian deli. Rosemary
and raisins together are a marriage made in heaven
and adding a scattering caster sugar over the cake
batter before baking creates a whisper of crisp, sugary
crust as it cooks. Awesome. Two pieces for me please.

Preheat the oven to 180°C/350°F/gas mark 4. Cream the
butter and sugar together until light and fluffy. Add the eggs,
a little at a time, stirring in between each addition, until the
mixture is smooth and all the eggs are incorporated.

Add the flour, followed by the rosemary and raisins and
stir well until everything is smoothly incorporated.

Spoon the mixture into the prepared tin and sprinkle
the top evenly with the extra caster sugar before baking
for 40 minutes, or until the cake is golden and springy.
Allow to cool in the tin, then cut into squares. Store in
an airtight container.

Plum Frangipane Slices

Makes 15
Preparation time: 1 hour and 10 minutes,
plus 30 minutes resting for the pastry
You will need a Swiss roll tin measuring
23 x 30 cm/9 x 12 inches

Pastry
175 g/6 oz butter
50 g/1¾ oz caster sugar, plus extra for sprinkling
1 egg yolk
320 g/11 oz plain flour, sifted

Frangipane
400 g/14 oz butter
400 g/14 oz sugar
4 eggs, beaten
400 g/14 oz ground almonds
4 tablespoons plain flour, sifted

1 kg/2 lb 2 oz plums, halved and stoned

This gorgeous almond affair sets rows of sweet juicy plums in moist frangipane. This is a big bake and one to please a crowd or cut up and freeze between layers of greaseproof paper to bring out and defrost as needed. Occasionally the filling might bubble lava-like towards the edges of the tin, not quite spilling over but creating a chewy, marzipan-like frame around the edges. In the interests of neatness, trim this off.

To make the pastry, cream the butter and sugar together until light and smooth and then beat in the egg yolk. Add the flour, and bring the mixture together to form a smooth pastry dough. Wrap the pastry in plastic wrap and chill in the fridge for 30 minutes.

To make the frangipane, beat the butter and sugar together until smooth, and then add the eggs. Stir in the ground almonds and the flour, and then beat until smooth.

Preheat the oven to 180°C/350°F/gas mark 4. Roll the pastry out to cover the base of the tin and trim the edges neatly. Spread the frangipane evenly over the pastry. Gently push the plums, cut side up, into the frangipane at even intervals. Bake for 40–50 minutes or so, until the topping is golden and springy to the touch.

Leave to cool in the tin, sprinkle with a little caster sugar and cut into squares or slices. Store in an airtight container.

Variation:
Ring the changes by substituting other fresh fruit when in season. Stone fruit such as cherries, apricots and peaches (stone removed of course) are all sublime – as are raspberries, grapes and a personal favourite of mine – the physalis or Cape gooseberry. Firm tinned fruits such as pears are perfect (and quick) to use too.

Ricotta Slices

Makes 15
Preparation time: 1 hour and 10 minutes,
plus 30 minutes resting for the pastry
You will need a Swiss roll tin measuring
23 x 30 cm/9 x 12 inches

Pastry
175 g/6 oz butter
50 g/1¾ oz caster sugar
1 egg yolk
320 g/11 oz plain flour, sifted

Topping
750 g/1 lb 10 oz ricotta
300 g/10 oz sugar
zest and juice of 1 lemon
4 eggs, beaten
50 g/1¾ oz ground almonds
100 g/3½ oz currants
freshly grated nutmeg

To make the pastry, cream the butter with the sugar until
light and smooth and then beat in the egg yolk. Add the
flour, and bring the mixture together to form a smooth
pastry dough. Wrap the pastry in plastic wrap and chill in
the fridge for 30 minutes.

Preheat the oven to 180°C/350°F/gas mark 4. To make the
topping, beat the ricotta, sugar, lemon zest and juice together
with the eggs. Stir in the ground almonds and currants.

Roll the pastry out to cover the base of the tin and trim
the edges neatly. Spoon the ricotta mixture evenly over the
pastry base and sprinkle with a little grated nutmeg. Bake for
40 minutes or so, until the topping is golden and set.

Leave to cool in the tin and then cut into slices. Store
them in airtight container.

Chocolate Chip Squares

Makes 15
Preparation time: 1 hour
You will need a lightly buttered deep roasting tin
or cake tin measuring 20 x 30 cm/8 x 12 inches

250 g/9 oz butter
250 g/9 oz caster sugar
4 eggs, beaten
250 g/9 oz self-raising flour
50 g/1¾ oz cocoa powder
150 g/5 oz plain chocolate chips

Preheat the oven to 180°C/350°F/gas mark 4. Cream the
butter and sugar together until light and fluffy. Add the eggs,
a little at a time, stirring, until the mixture is smooth and all
the eggs are incorporated. You may have to add a little flour
in between each addition to prevent the mixture curdling.

Sift the remaining flour and cocoa powder together then
stir them into the creamed mixture. Add the chocolate chips.
Spoon into the prepared tin and bake for 30 minutes, or
until golden and springy. Cool in the tin and cut into
squares. Store in an airtight container.

Variation:
For a slight variation, add a hint of orange by stirring the
grated zest of 1 large orange into the cake mixture before
baking. Or, as a lovely alternative to the dark chocolate chips,
add 1 teaspoon of real vanilla extract and substitute white
chocolate chips, or a combination of both white and milk.

Iced Coffee Squares

Makes 15
Preparation time: 1 hour
You will need a lightly buttered deep roasting tin or cake tin measuring 20 x 30 cm/8 x 12 inches

250 g/9 oz butter
250 g/9 oz sugar
4 eggs, beaten
250 g/9 oz self-raising flour
50 ml/2 fl oz espresso coffee

Icing
300 g/10 oz icing sugar
small espresso coffee

Preheat the oven to 180°C/350°F/gas mark 4. Cream the butter and sugar together until pale and fluffy and then beat in the eggs, a little at a time until the mixture is smooth. You may have to add a little flour in between each addition to prevent curdling. When the eggs are fully incorporated, add the remaining flour. Stir in the espresso. Spoon into the prepared tin and bake for 50 minutes or so, until risen and golden. Cool in the tin.

Meanwhile, make the icing by mixing the icing sugar with enough of the espresso to make a consistency similar to that of thick pouring cream. Pour over the cake and leave to set. Cut into squares and store in an airtight container.

Iced Cherry and Almond Squares

Makes 15
Preparation time: 1 hour and 10 minutes, plus cooling
You will need a lightly buttered deep roasting tin or cake tin measuring 20 x 30 cm/8 x 12 inches

200 g/7 oz glacé cherries, halved
150 g/5 oz plain flour
250 g/9 oz butter
350 g/12 oz caster sugar
6 eggs, lightly beaten
150 g/5 oz ground almonds
1 teaspoon almond essence

Icing
300 g/10 oz icing sugar
3–4 tablespoons water

Preheat the oven to 180°C/350°F/gas mark 4. Rinse the cherries and dry them thoroughly. Toss in a little flour to ensure they are no longer sticky.

Cream the butter and sugar together until pale and fluffy and then beat in the eggs, a little at a time until the mixture is smooth. You may have to add a little flour in between each addition to prevent curdling. Stir in the remaining flour, the ground almonds and almond essence. Fold in the cherries. Spoon into the prepared tin. Bake for 40–45 minutes or so, until risen and golden. Cool in the tin.

Meanwhile, make the icing by mixing the icing sugar with enough water to make a consistency similar to thick pouring cream. Pour over the cake and leave to set. Cut into squares and store in an airtight container.

Bakewell Slices

Makes 15
Preparation time: 1 hour, plus 30 minutes
resting for the pastry
You will need a Swiss roll tin measuring
23 x 30 cm/9 x 12 inches

Pastry
175 g/6 oz butter
50 g/1¾ oz caster sugar
1 egg yolk
320 g/11 oz plain flour, sifted
500 g/1 lb 2 oz raspberry jam

Topping
200 g/7 oz almonds
200 g/7 oz semolina
200 g/7 oz caster sugar
4 eggs
200 g/7 oz butter, melted
icing sugar, for dusting

To make the pastry, cream the butter and sugar together
until light and smooth and then beat in the egg yolk. Add
the flour, and bring the mixture together to form a smooth
pastry dough. Wrap the pastry in plastic wrap and chill in
the fridge for 30 minutes.

Preheat the oven to 180°C/350°F/gas mark 4. Roll the
pastry out to cover the base of the tin and trim the edges
neatly. Spread the jam evenly over the pastry.

To make the topping, place the almonds, semolina and
sugar in a bowl and stir in the eggs. Add the melted butter
and beat until smooth. Spread evenly over the jam. Bake for
25–30 minutes, until golden and firm to the touch.

Dust with icing sugar. Cool in the tin and cut into slices.
Store in an airtight container.

Earl Grey Tea Squares

Makes 15
Preparation time: 2 hours, including soaking
You will need a lightly buttered deep roasting tin
or cake tin measuring 20 x 30 cm/8 x 12 inches

200 g/7 oz sultanas
150 ml/5 fl oz freshly made Earl Grey tea
250 g/9 oz butter
250 g/9 oz caster sugar
4 eggs, lightly beaten
250 g/9 oz self raising flour

Icing
300 g/10 oz icing sugar
30 g/1 oz butter, melted
reserved tea (see method)

Preheat the oven to 180°C/350°F/gas mark 4. Soak the
sultanas in the tea for an hour or so.

Cream the butter and sugar together until they become
pale and fluffy and then add the eggs, a little at a time,
until fully incorporated. Add the flour. Drain the sultanas
(reserving the tea) and stir them evenly through the mixture.
Spoon into the prepared tin and bake for 45 minutes, until
golden and springy to the touch. Leave to cool in the tin.

Meanwhile, make the icing by mixing the icing sugar
with the butter and enough of the reserved tea to make a
consistency similar to that of thick pouring cream. Drizzle
over the cake and leave to set. Cut the cake into squares and
store in an airtight containere.

Pistachio and Almond Bars

Makes 15
Preparation time: 1 hour and 20 minutes, plus cooling
You will need a lightly buttered deep roasting tin or
cake tin measuring 20 x 30 cm/8 x 12 inches

250 g/9 oz butter
350 g/12 oz caster sugar
6 eggs, lightly beaten
150 g/5 oz plain flour
150 g/5 oz ground almonds
1 teaspoon almond essence

Topping
300 g/10 oz white chocolate, chopped
150 g/5 oz pistachios, cut into slivers

Preheat the oven to 180°C/350°F/gas mark 4. Cream the
butter and sugar together until pale and fluffy and then beat
in the eggs, a little at a time until the mixture is smooth.
You may have to add a little flour in between each addition
to prevent curdling. Stir in the remaining flour, the ground
almonds and almond essence. Spoon into the prepared tin
and bake for 50 minutes or so, until risen and golden.
Allow to cool in the tin.

Once the cake is cold, make the topping by melting the
chocolate in a bowl over a saucepan of gently simmering
water. (Alternatively microwave on high for 1 minute.)
Spread over the cake. Scatter over the pistachios and set
aside until the chocolate sets. Cut into squares and store
in an airtight container in a cool place.

Banana Chip and Coconut Flapjacks

Preparation time: 40 minutes
Makes 12
You will need a roasting tin or shallow tin measuring
20 x 25 cm/8 x 10 inches

200 g/7 oz butter
200 g/7 oz light brown sugar
5 tablespoons golden syrup
375 g/13 oz whole porridge oats
50 g/1¾ oz desiccated coconut
100 g/3½ oz dried banana chips, crushed

Crunchy dried banana chips make these fabulous
flapjacks popular with all ages. Many years ago, I used
to bake brownies and bars for a local coffee shop and
one particular lady used to buy two of these every day.
And every day without fail, she would ask me for the
recipe. Eventually I gave it to her – and that was the
last time she came into the shop! Needless to say,
my little act of munificence didn't go down too well
with the owners, so apart from sharing it with a
friend or two, I've kept the recipe to myself ever since.
Until now, that is.

Preheat the oven to 180°C/350°F/gas mark 4. Melt the
butter, sugar and golden syrup in a saucepan over a gentle
heat. (Alternatively, microwave on the highest setting for
1–2 minutes.) Stir in the oats, coconut and banana chips.
Spoon the mixture into the tin and bake for 25 minutes,
or until golden and firm.

Cool for 10 minutes or so and then mark into bars.
Leave the flapjacks to cool completely before lifting them
out of the tin. Store in an airtight container.

Iced Cherry Slices

Makes 15
Preparation time: 1 hour, plus 30 minutes
resting for the pastry
You will need a Swiss roll tin measuring
23 x 30 cm/9 x 12 inches

Pastry
175 g/6 oz butter
50 g/1¾ oz caster sugar
1 egg yolk
320 g/11 oz plain flour, sifted
450 g/1 lb cherry jam

Topping
175 g/6 oz butter
175 g/6 oz caster sugar
3 eggs, beaten
175 g/6 oz self-raising flour
400 g/14 oz icing sugar

Delicious, light pastry with a slick of cherry jam make these iced slices a simple everyday treat. Aim to use the best jam you can find. Homemade is ideal, but ready-made is perfectly fine too.

To make the pastry, cream the butter and sugar together until light and smooth and then beat in the egg yolk. Add the flour, and bring the mixture together to form a smooth pastry dough. Wrap the pastry in plastic wrap and chill in the fridge for 30 minutes.

Preheat the oven to 180°C/350°F/gas mark 4. Roll the pastry out to cover the base of the tin and trim the edges neatly. Spread the jam evenly over the pastry.

To make the topping, beat the butter and sugar together until light and fluffy. Stir in the eggs, and then add the flour and beat until smooth. Spread evenly over the jam and bake for 20–25 minutes, until golden and springy to the touch. Leave to cool in the tin.

Sift the icing sugar into a bowl and add enough water to make a consistency similar to that of thick pouring cream. Spread over the sponge and leave to set. Cut into slices and store in an airtight container.

Crunchy Oat Flapjacks

Preparation time: 40 minutes
Makes 12
You will need a roasting tin or shallow tin measuring
20 x 25 cm/8 x 10 inches

180 g/6½ oz butter
180 g/6½ oz light brown sugar
4 tablespoons golden syrup
375 g/13 oz whole porridge oats
50 g/1¾ oz cornflakes

Tara Fisher, who photographed this book, says that these are the best flapjacks she has ever tasted. Thank you Tara. My son Tim loves them too – especially accompanied by a tall glass of ice-cold creamy milk to recharge the batteries after a long day at school. Using whole oats rather than rolled porridge oats gives them a dangerously addictive, deliciously chewy texture.

Preheat the oven to 180°C/350°F/gas mark 4. Gently melt the butter, brown sugar and golden syrup together in a saucepan set over a low heat. (Alternatively, microwave on high for 1–2 minutes.)

Gently stir in the whole porridge oats and cornflakes, taking care not to break them up too much. Spoon the mixture into the baking tin.

Bake for 25 minutes, or until the flapjacks have turned golden and become firm.

Remove from the oven and allow to cool for 10 minutes or so and then cut into bars. Leave the flapjacks to cool completely before lifting them out of the tin. Store in an airtight container.

Variation:
A handful of raisins (about 85 g/3 oz) makes an excellent, juicy addition to these flapjacks. A tablespoon of toasted sunflower seeds adds an extra crunchy dimension.

Almond Slices

Makes 15
Preparation time: 1 hour, plus 30 minutes
resting for the pastry
You will need a Swiss roll tin measuring
23 x 30 cm/9 x 12 inches

Pastry
175 g/6 oz butter
50 g/1¾ oz caster sugar
1 egg yolk
320 g/11 oz plain flour, sifted
500 g/1 lb 2 oz raspberry jam

Topping
200 g/7 oz almonds
200 g/7 oz semolina
200 g/7 oz caster sugar, plus extra for sprinkling
4 eggs, beaten
1 teaspoon almond essence
250 g/9 oz butter, melted
100 g/3½ oz flaked almonds

To make the pastry, cream the butter and sugar together until light and smooth and then beat in the egg yolk. Add the flour, and bring the mixture together to form a smooth pastry dough. Wrap the pastry in plastic wrap and chill in the fridge for 30 minutes.

Preheat the oven to 180°C/350°F/gas mark 4. Roll the pastry out to cover the base of the tin and trim the edges neatly. Spread the jam evenly over the pastry.

To make the topping, place the almonds, semolina and sugar in a bowl and stir in the eggs. Add the almond essence and the melted butter and beat until smooth. Spread the mixture evenly over the jam and scatter with flaked almonds.

Bake for 25–30 minutes, or until golden and firm to the touch. Sprinkle with caster sugar and leave to cool in the tin. Cut into slices. Store in an airtight container.

Easy Orange Cake

Makes 15
Preparation time: 2 hours, including cooling and icing
You will need a lightly buttered, deep roasting pan or cake tin measuring 20 x 30 cm/8 x 12 inches

250 g/9 oz butter
250 g/9 oz caster sugar
4 eggs
250 g/9 oz self-raising flour
grated zest of 1 large orange

Icing
400 g/14 oz icing sugar
juice of 1 large orange
grated zest of 1 orange

Preheat the oven to 180°C/350°F/gas mark 4. Cream the butter and sugar together until light and fluffy. Add the eggs, a little at a time, stirring in between each addition, until the mixture is smooth and all the eggs are incorporated.

Add the flour and the orange zest and beat until smooth. Spoon the mixture into the prepared tin and bake for 40 minutes or so, until the cake is golden and springy. Leave to cool in the tin.

Meanwhile, sieve the icing sugar into a large bowl and mix with enough of the orange juice to make an icing with the consistency of thick cream. When the cake is completely cold, spread the top with a layer of the icing and scatter with orange zest. Cut the cake into squares and store in an airtight container.

Mango and Pistachio Bars

Makes 15
Preparation time: 45 minutes, plus cooling
You will need a lightly buttered deep roasting tin
or cake tin measuring 20 x 30 cm/8 x 12 inches

500 g/1 lb 2 oz oat biscuits, such as Anzac biscuits, crushed
200 g/7 oz desiccated coconut
400 g/14 oz dried mango, chopped
200 g/7 oz pistachios, cut into slivers
400 ml/14 fl oz condensed milk
200 g/7 oz butter, melted
3 tablespoons Malibu (coconut) liqueur (optional)

Icing
150 g/5 oz butter
400 g/14 oz icing sugar
2–3 tablespoons Malibu (coconut) liqueur
4–5 tablespoons flaked coconut, lightly toasted

Preheat the oven to 180°C/350°F/gas mark 4. Put the biscuits in a large bowl with the coconut, mango and pistachios. Stir in the condensed milk, butter, and Malibu, if using. Spoon the mixture into the prepared tin and bake for 25 minutes, or until golden and springy. Leave to cool in the tin.

To make the icing, beat the butter and icing sugar together with the Malibu and spread over the cooled cake. Scatter with the flaked coconut and cut into bars. Store in an airtight container.

Bread Pudding

Makes 15
Preparation time: 1 hour and 10 minutes, plus
30 minutes soaking
You will need a lightly buttered deep roasting tin
or cake tin measuring 20 x 30 cm/8 x 12 inches

500 g/1 lb 2 oz white bread, crusts removed
600 ml/1 pint milk
1 tablespoon mixed spice
2 eggs, beaten
100 g/3½ oz butter, melted
175 g/6 oz light muscovado sugar

Topping
4–5 tablespoons good quality apricot jam, sieved
caster sugar, for sprinkling

Bread pudding was originally born out of thrift, possibly some time in the 18th century. Soaking tired bread and baking it with a mix of fruit, spices, sugar and eggs was the frugal cook's way of making something sweet and tasty from something past its best. Whenever I see bread pudding sold locally in cake shops, it always seems to come in Sumo-size slices. Not so here. This recipe yields fifteen squares of far more delicate dimensions.

Cut the bread into rough pieces and soak in the milk for 30 minutes. Preheat the oven to 180°C/350°F/gas mark 4.

Beat the bread and milk together until smooth. Stir in the remaining ingredients and spoon the mixture into the prepared tin. Bake for 1 hour, until firm and golden.

Leave to cool in the tin, brush with apricot jam, sprinkle with caster sugar and then cut into squares. Store in an airtight container.

Toffee and Hazelnut Shortbread Crumble Bars

Makes 16
Preparation time: 1 hour
You will need a Swiss roll tin measuring
23 x 30 cm/9 x 12 inches

Shortbread
300 g/10½ oz butter
300 g/10½ plain flour
200 g/7 oz ground rice
200 g/7 oz sugar
100 g/3½ oz hazelnuts, toasted and chopped

Topping
800 ml/1¼ pints condensed milk
200 g/7 oz butter
200 g/7 oz sugar
500 g/1 lb 2 oz (drained weight) canned pineapple chunks

These bars come from the Banoffee pie camp, but are made with chewy toffee and chunks of juicy pineapple, then finished off with a crumbly golden hazelnut topping. They're definitely for toffee lovers and those with a seriously sweet-tooth.

Preheat the oven to 180°C/350°F/gas mark 4. To make the shortbread, rub the butter, flour and ground rice together and then add the sugar. Squeeze half of the mixture lightly together to form a ball and press it into the prepared tin. Bake for 20 minutes, until golden and firm to the touch. Remove from the oven and set aside. Add the chopped hazelnuts to the remaining mixture.

To make the topping, pour the condensed milk into a heavy-based saucepan and add the butter and sugar. Stir over a medium heat until the butter has melted and the sugar is completely dissolved. Turn down the heat and bubble for 10 minutes or so, until thick, golden and fudge-like.

Spread the topping evenly over the shortbread base and scatter over the pineapple chunks. Sprinkle the crumbly hazelnut mixture on top and return to the oven for 10–15 minutes, until the topping is golden and crisp.

Leave to cool in the tin. Cut into bars and store in an airtight container in a cool place.

Note:
These bars work beautifully if frozen between layers of greaseproof paper and then lifted out individually and defrosted as needed. Simply leave them at room temperature for an hour or so and then serve.

For an almost instant dessert, set the oven to a low heat, remove the bars from the freezer and pop them in the oven on a baking sheet until defrosted and warmed through. Serve immediately with a generous dollop of vanilla ice cream,

Fudgy Lemon Bars

Makes 25
Preparation time: 45 minutes, plus 30 minutes
resting for the pastry
You will need a deep roasting tin or cake tin
measuring 20 x 25 cm/8 x 10 inches

Base
200 g/7 oz butter
200 g/7 oz plain flour
100 g/3½ oz cornflour
100 g/3½ oz sugar

Fudgy lemon topping
600 ml/1 pint double cream
300 g/10 oz caster sugar
4 eggs
100 g/3½ oz plain flour
zest and juice of 3 large unwaxed lemons

These dangerously addictive lemon bars are wildly
moreish. I have to draw on every ounce of willpower
to stop at one (and seldom do). It's essential that the
cold lemon mixture be poured straight onto the hot
shortbread as soon as it comes out of the oven, the
whole thing then needs to be returned to the oven
immediately, or the lemon mixture will simply soak
into the base and become soggy. I sometimes use a
slightly smaller tray, which produces somewhat
deeper, even fudgier bars.

To make the base, rub the butter, plain flour and cornflour
together until the mixture resembles fine breadcrumbs.
Add the sugar and bring the mixture together to form a
smooth, soft dough. Wrap in plastic wrap and refrigerate
for 30 minutes.

Preheat the oven to 180°C/350°F/gas mark 4. Roll the
dough out to line the baking tin. Bake for 10–15 minutes,
or until golden in colour.

Meanwhile, make the topping by whisking the cream,
sugar and eggs together. Add the flour, lemon zest and lemon
juice and continue to whisk until the mixture is smooth and
light. Remove the cooked shortbread base from the oven and
IMMEDIATELY pour on the lemon mixture. Return to the
oven and bake for 20–25 minutes, until the topping is set.

Remove from the oven and leave to cool completely. Dust
lightly with caster sugar and cut into slices or bars. Store in
an airtight container in a cool place.

Lemon and Almond Bars

Makes 15
Preparation time: 1 hour, plus optional 30 minutes
resting for pastry
You will need a lightly buttered Swiss roll tin
measuring 23 x 30 cm/9 x 12 inches

Pastry
175 g/6 oz butter
50 g/1¾ oz caster sugar
1 egg yolk
320 g/11 oz plain flour, sifted
400 g/14 oz lemon curd

Topping
175 g/6 oz butter
175 g/6 oz caster sugar, plus extra for dusting
3 eggs, beaten
175 g/6 oz self-raising flour
50 g/1¾ oz flaked almonds

To make the pastry, cream the butter and sugar together until
light and smooth and then beat in the egg yolk. Add the
flour, and bring the mixture together to form a smooth
pastry dough. Wrap the pastry in plastic wrap and chill in
the fridge for 30 minutes.

Preheat the oven to 180°C/350°F/gas mark 4. Roll the
pastry out to cover the base of the prepared tin and trim the
edges neatly. Spread the lemon curd evenly over the pastry.

To make the topping, cream the butter and sugar together
until light and fluffy. Stir in the eggs, and then add the flour
and beat until smooth. Spread evenly over the lemon curd.
Sprinkle over the almonds and bake for 20–25 minutes,
until golden and springy to the touch. Leave to cool.

Dust with caster sugar. Cool in the tin and cut into bars.
Store in an airtight container.

Spiced Gingerbread Bars

Makes 15
Preparation time: 1 hour
You will need a lightly buttered deep roasting tin or
cake tin measuring 20 x 30 cm/8 x 12 inches

320 g/11 oz plain flour
2 tablespoons bicarbonate of soda
2 teaspoons ground ginger
2 teaspoons ground cinnamon
400 g/14 oz light muscovado sugar
180 g/6¼ oz butter
100 ml/4 fl oz milk
250 ml/9 fl oz soured cream
2 eggs, beaten
6 pieces stem ginger, roughly chopped

Here's a simple cake with just the right amount of
ginger, an airy lightness and a lovely open texture.
It tastes just as good on a picnic rug as it does at the
kitchen table with a pot of tea.

Preheat the oven to 180°C/350°F/gas mark 4. Sift the flour,
bicarbonate of soda and spices into a large bowl and then stir
in the sugar.

Place the butter and milk in a saucepan and heat gently
until the butter has melted. Pour the mixture into the flour
mixture and stir well until thoroughly combined. Add the
soured cream and eggs, and then stir in the stem ginger.
Pour into the prepared tin and bake for 45 minutes or so,
until golden and springy. Leave to cool then cut into bars
and store in an airtight container.

Prune Breton Bars

Makes 14
Preparation time: 2 hours and 30 minutes, including resting the dough
You will need a lightly buttered, shallow roasting pan or cake tin measuring 20 x 30 cm/8 x 12 inches

Dough
450 g/1 lb plain flour
300 g/3½ oz butter, softened
225 g/8 oz caster sugar
6 egg yolks
1 tablespoon rum

Filling
450 g/1 lb good quality prune jam

Glaze
1 egg yolk, beaten

These buttery prune-filled bars are based on the French speciality Gateau Breton – a delicious creation that is traditionally served unadorned and relies almost entirely on the quality of the butter for its lovely flavour. I tasted a version in Brittany that had a thin layer of prune purée in the centre and loved it; this recipe is based on that.

Preheat the oven to 190°C/370°F/gas mark 5. Place all of the ingredients for the dough together in a food processor and mix until you have a very soft but smooth dough. Form the dough into a ball and chill in the refrigerator for 1 hour.

Press half of the dough evenly into the prepared tin. Spread with the prune jam and carefully cover the prune jam with the remaining dough. Brush the dough with the egg yolk and score the surface of the dough with the tines of a fork to create an attractive pattern.

Bake for 15 minutes, and then turn the oven temperature down to 180°C/350°F/gas mark 4 and cook for a further 35–40 minutes, or until firm and golden. Leave to cool in the tin, and then cut into squares or diamonds and store in an airtight container.

Lemon Coconut Squares

Makes 15
Preparation time: 1 hour, plus cooling
You will need a lightly buttered deep roasting tin
or cake tin measuring 20 x 30 cm/8 x 12 inches

250 g/9 oz butter
250 g/9 oz caster sugar
4 eggs, beaten
300 g/10 oz self-raising flour
2 tablespoons lemon curd

Coating
300 g/10 oz lemon curd
200 g/7 oz desiccated coconut

Preheat the oven to 180°C/350°F/gas mark 4. Cream the
butter and sugar together until pale and fluffy and then
beat in the eggs, a little at a time until the mixture is smooth.
When the eggs are fully incorporated, add the flour and then
stir in the lemon curd. Spoon into the prepared tin and bake
for 40 minutes or so, until risen and golden.

Cool in the tin. Cut the cooled cake into squares, spread
each side with lemon curd and roll in the coconut to coat
all sides. Store in an airtight container.

Golden Pear and Thyme Cake

Makes 15
Preparation time: 1 hour and 20 minutes
You will need a lightly buttered, deep roasting pan
or cake tin measuring 20 x 30 cm/8 x 12 inches

280 g/10 oz butter
280 g/10 oz caster sugar
4 firm, but ripe pears, peeled, cored and diced
4 eggs
250 g/9 oz self-raising flour, sifted
1 tablespoon thyme leaves
1 tablespoon caster sugar, for sprinkling

Set the oven to 180°C/350°F/gas mark 4. Heat 30 g/1 oz of
butter and 30 g/1 oz of the sugar together in a pan, until the
sugar has dissolved. Add the diced pear and cook for about
5 minutes, until the pear is golden and caramelised. Leave to
cool slightly.

Cream the remaining butter and sugar together until light
and fluffy. Add the eggs, a little at a time, stirring in between
each addition, until the mixture is smooth and all the eggs
are incorporated.

Add the flour, and then stir in the cooled pears with any
buttery juices, and the thyme. Spoon the mixture into the
prepared tin and bake for 40 minutes, or until the cake is
golden and springy. Allow the cake to cool in the tin, scatter
with the extra caster sugar, and then cut into squares. Store
in an airtight container.

Something Sticky

Chocolate, Pear and Macadamia Nut Brownies

Makes 15
Preparation time: 55 minutes
You will need a lightly buttered deep roasting tin or cake tin measuring 20 x 30 cm/8 x 12 inches

250 g/9 oz butter
500 g/1 lb 2 oz caster sugar
100 g/3½ oz cocoa powder
4 eggs, beaten
100 g/3½ oz self-raising flour
2 ripe but firm pears, peeled, cored and diced
100 g/3½ oz macadamia nuts, roughly chopped

Preheat the oven to 180°C/350°F/gas mark 4. Place the butter, sugar and cocoa in a saucepan set over a gentle heat and stir until the butter has melted. (Alternatively, you can microwave on high for a minute or so.) Leave to cool a little.

Beat the eggs into the cocoa mixture. Stir in the flour, followed by the pears and macadamia nuts. Pour the mixture into the prepared tin and bake for 25 minutes, or until the brownies are just set, taking care not to overcook them – the texture should be fudgy rather than cakey.

Leave to cool in the tin and cut into square or bars. Store in an airtight container.

Chocolate and Pistachio Brownies

Makes 15
Preparation time: 45 minutes
You will need a lightly buttered deep roasting tin or cake tin measuring 20 x 30 cm/8 x 12 inches

250 g/9 oz butter
500 g/1 lb 2oz caster sugar
100 g/3½ oz cocoa powder
4 eggs, beaten
100 g/3½ oz self-raising flour
150 g/5 oz pistachios

Preheat the oven to 180°C/350°F/gas mark 4. Place the butter, sugar and cocoa in a saucepan over a gentle heat and stir until the butter has melted. (Alternatively, microwave on high for a minute or so.) Leave the mixture to cool a little.

Beat the eggs into the cocoa mixture. Stir in the flour and pistachios and pour into the prepared tin. Bake for 25 minutes or so, until the brownies are just set. Take care not to overcook them – the texture should be fudgy rather than cake-like.

Leave to cool in the tin and cut into square or bars. Store in an airtight container.

Banana and Nutmeg Custard Brownies

Makes 15
Preparation time: 1½ hours
You will need a lightly buttered roasting tin or cake tin measuring 20 x 30 cm/8 x 10 inches

250 g/9 oz butter
500 g/1 lb 2 oz caster sugar
125 g/4½ oz cocoa powder
4 eggs, beaten
100 g/3½ oz self-raising flour
2 bananas, mashed

Custard layer
250 g/9 oz mascarpone
4 egg yolks
100 g/3½ oz caster sugar
freshly grated nutmeg

Dense fudgy chocolate-and-banana brownie on the bottom, creamy nutmeg spiked custard on the top. Cloud nine stuff really. Make sure to use VERY ripe bananas – the sort that look quite speckled and brown (although take care that their colour is due to ripeness not bruising). They'll be oozing big banana flavour and a natural sweetness that will add unbelievable flavour.

Preheat the oven to 180°C/350°F/gas mark 4. Melt the butter, sugar and cocoa powder together in a pan set over a low heat. Remove from the heat and leave to cool slightly.

Stir the eggs into the cocoa mixture and fold in the flour. Stir in the mashed banana and spoon the mixture into the prepared tin.

To make the custard layer, whisk the mascarpone, egg yolks and sugar together until smooth and then carefully drizzle randomly over the chocolate banana mixture. Sprinkle the custard with a little grated nutmeg and bake for 35 minutes or so, until just firm but still slightly fudgy.

Leave to cool in the tin and then cut into squares. Store in an airtight container in a cool place.

Espresso Brownies

Makes 15
Preparation time: 45 minutes
You will need a lightly buttered deep roasting tin or cake tin measuring 20 x 30 cm/8 x 12 inches

250 g/9 oz butter
500 g/1lb 2oz caster sugar
100 g/3½ oz dark chocolate
50 g/1¾ oz cocoa powder
4 eggs, beaten
100 g/3½ oz self-raising flour
2 tablespoons strong espresso coffee
2 tablespoons coffee beans, lightly crushed

Preheat the oven to 180°C/350°F/gas mark 4. Place the butter, sugar, chocolate and cocoa together in a saucepan set over a gentle heat and stir until the butter has melted. (Alternatively, microwave on high for a minute or so.) Leave the mixture to cool a little.

Beat the eggs into the chocolate mixture, then stir in the flour and espresso. Pour into the prepared tin and scatter the crushed coffee beans over the top. Bake for 25 minutes, or until the brownies are just set. Be careful not to overcook them – the texture should be fudgy.

Leave to cool in the tin and then cut into square or bars. Store in an airtight container.

Sticky Toffee Squares

Makes 15
Preparation time: 1 hour, plus 30 minutes soaking
You will need a lightly buttered deep roasting tin or cake tin measuring 20 x 30 cm/8 x 12 inches

150 g/5 oz dried unsulphured apricots
4 tablespoons ginger wine
250 g/9 oz butter
500 g/1 lb 2 oz muscovado sugar
12 pieces stem ginger, finely chopped
4 eggs, beaten
1 tablespoon ground ginger
250 g/9 oz self-raising flour
1 teaspoon bicarbonate of soda
100 g/3½ oz walnuts, toasted and chopped
180 ml/12 tablespoons stem ginger syrup

Preheat the oven to 180°C/350°F/gas mark 4. Cut the apricots into small pieces. Pour over the ginger wine and leave to soak for 30 minutes or longer.

Place the butter and sugar into a saucepan and heat gently until melted (this can be done in a microwave). Turn the mixture into a large bowl and stir in the stem ginger, eggs and ground ginger. Sift the flour and bicarbonate of soda together and stir into the mixture until well mixed. Fold in the apricots and their soaking liquid, together with the chopped walnuts.

Pour into the prepared tin and bake for 30–35 minutes, until risen and firm but springy in the centre. Leave to cool. Pour over the ginger syrup and leave to soak in. Cut into squares and store in an airtight container.

Treacle Slices

Makes 15
Preparation time: 1 hour, plus 30 minutes resting for the pastry
You will need a Swiss roll tin measuring 23 x 32 cm/ 9 x 12 inches

Pastry
175 g/6 oz butter
50 g/1¾ oz caster sugar
1 egg yolk
320 g/11 oz plain flour, sifted

Topping
500 g/1 lb 2 oz golden syrup
1 egg, beaten
4 tablespoons double cream
3 tablespoons brandy
100 g/3½ oz breadcrumbs

To make the pastry, cream the butter and sugar together until light and smooth and then beat in the egg yolk. Add the flour, and bring the mixture together to form a smooth pastry dough. Wrap the pastry in plastic wrap and chill in the fridge for 30 minutes.

Preheat the oven to 180°C/350°F/gas mark 4. Lightly flour a work surface, roll out slightly less than half the pastry and use to line the baking tin.

To make the topping, mix the golden syrup, egg, cream and brandy together, and then stir in the breadcrumbs. Pour into the pastry case and bake for 30 minutes or so, until set and golden.

Set aside to cool, then cut into slices and store in an airtight container.

Sticky Pecan Slices

Makes 15
Preparation time: 1 hour and 10 minutes, plus
30 minutes resting for the pastry
You will need a Swiss roll tin measuring 23 x 30 cm/
9 x 12 inches

Pastry
175 g/6 oz butter
50 g/1¾ oz caster sugar
1 egg yolk
320 g/11 oz plain flour, sifted

Topping
6 eggs, beaten
450 ml/15 fl oz maple syrup
200 g/7 oz muscovado sugar
300 g/10 oz butter, melted
300 g/10 oz pecan nuts

To make the pastry, cream the butter and sugar together
until light and smooth and then beat in the egg yolk. Add
the flour, and bring the mixture together to form a smooth
pastry dough. If time allows, wrap the pastry in plastic wrap
and chill in the fridge for 30 minutes.

Preheat the oven to 180°C/350°F/gas mark 4. Roll the
pastry out until it is large enough to cover the base of the
tin, then trim the edges neatly.

Beat the eggs, maple syrup, sugar and butter together until
smooth. Stir in the nuts. Pour over the pastry base and bake
for 35 minutes or so, until golden and set.

Allow to cool in the tin and then cut into bars. Store in an
airtight container.

Pine Nut and Almond Bars

Makes 16
Preparation time: 1 hour and 10 minutes, plus
optional 30 minutes resting for pastry
You will need a Swiss roll tin measuring 23 x 30 cm/
9 x 12 inches

Pastry
175 g/6 oz butter
50 g/1¾ oz caster sugar
1 egg yolk
320 g/11 oz plain flour, sifted

Topping
4 eggs, beaten
300 ml/½ pint golden syrup
150 g/5 oz butter, melted
zest 1 lemon
100 g/3½ oz pine nuts
100 g/3½ oz flaked almonds
100 g/3½ oz cornflakes

To make the pastry, cream the butter and sugar together until
they become light and smooth and then beat in the egg yolk.
Add the flour, and bring the mixture together to form a
smooth pastry dough. Wrap the pastry in plastic wrap and
chill in the fridge for 30 minutes.

Preheat the oven to 180°C/350°F/gas mark 4. Roll the
pastry out until it is large enough to cover the base of the
tin, then trim the edges neatly.

To make the topping, beat the eggs, golden syrup, butter
and lemon zest together. Stir in the nuts and cornflakes.
Pour over the pastry base and bake for 35 minutes, or until
golden and set.

Allow to cool in the tin and then cut into bars. Store in an
airtight container.

Chocolate and Orange Marble Squares

Makes 15
Preparation time: 1 hour and 10 minutes
You will need a lightly buttered deep roasting tin
or cake tin measuring 20 x 30 cm/8 x 12 inches

250 g/9 oz butter
250 g/9 oz sugar
4 eggs, beaten
250 g/9 oz self-raising flour, sifted
juice and zest 1 orange
3 tablespoons cocoa powder

Preheat the oven to 180°C/350°F/gas mark 4. Cream the
butter and sugar together until light and fluffy. Add the eggs,
a little at a time, stirring in between each addition, until the
mixture is smooth and all the eggs are incorporated. Stir in
the flour. Add the orange juice and zest. Spoon half of the
mixture in dollops randomly over the base of the prepared
cake tin.

   Add the cocoa powder to the remaining mixture and stir
until fully incorporated. Spoon the mixture in between the
dollops of orange mixture. Drag a wooden spoon handle
lightly through the mixtures to create a slight swirl effect.
Bake for 30–35 minutes or so, until golden and springy.

   Cool in the tin and cut into squares. Store them in an
airtight container.

Brandy and Apricot Brownies

Makes 15
Preparation time: 1 hour and 30 minutes, including
soaking the apricots
You will need a lightly buttered roasting pan or cake
tin measuring 20 x 30 cm/8 x 10 inches

50 g/2 oz dried apricots, chopped
3 tablespoons brandy
250 g/9 oz butter
500 g/1 lb 2 oz caster sugar
100 g/3½ oz cocoa powder
4 eggs, beaten
100 g/3½ oz self-raising flour
100 g/3½ oz pecan nuts, roughly chopped

I like to use unsulphered apricots for this recipe –
the brandy serves to emphasise their gorgeous dark
caramel flavour.

Pour the brandy over the apricots and leave them to soak for
30 minutes or so.

   Preheat the oven to 180°C/350°F/gas mark 4. Melt the
butter, sugar and cocoa powder together in a pan set over a
low heat. Remove from the heat and stir in the beaten eggs.
Fold in the flour, then stir in the apricots and the brandy in
which they have soaked. Add the pecans to the mixture,
then spoon into the prepared tin.

   Bake for 35 minutes, or until just firm but still slightly
fudgy. Allow to cool in the tin and then cut into squares.
Store in an airtight container.

Prune, Armagnac and Almond Brownies

Makes 15
Preparation time: 1 hour and 30 minutes, including soaking the prunes
You will need a lightly buttered roasting pan or cake tin measuring 20 x 30 cm/8 x 10 inches

85 g/3 oz dried prunes, chopped
3 tablespoons Armagnac

250 g/9 oz butter
500 g/1 lb 2 oz caster sugar
100 g/3½ oz cocoa powder
4 eggs, beaten
100 g/3½ oz self-raising flour
100 g/3½ oz blanched whole almonds, roughly chopped

Dark, sticky, dangerously addictive and fabulous with a scoop of real vanilla ice cream.

Pour the Armagnac over the prunes and leave them to soak for 30 minutes.

Preheat the oven to 180°C/350°F/gas mark 4. Melt the butter, sugar and cocoa powder together in a pan set over a low heat. Stir in the beaten eggs and fold in the flour. Stir in the prunes and the brandy in which they have soaked. Mix in the chopped almonds and spoon the mixture into the prepared tin.

Bake for 35 minutes or until just firm but still slightly fudgy. Allow to cool in the tin and then cut into squares. Store in an airtight container.

Chocolate Pecan Bars

Makes 15
Preparation time: 1¼ hours, plus optional 30 minutes resting for pastry
You will need a Swiss roll tin measuring 20 x 25 cm/ 8 x 10 inches

Pastry
175 g/6 oz butter
50 g/1¾ oz caster sugar
1 egg yolk
320 g/11 oz plain flour, sifted

Topping
200 g/7 oz chocolate
200 g/7 oz muscovado sugar
50 g/1¾ oz golden syrup
150 g/5 oz butter
4 eggs, beaten
200 g/7 oz pecan nuts

To make the pastry, cream the butter and sugar together until light and smooth and then beat in the egg yolk. Add the flour, and bring the mixture together to form a smooth pastry dough. If time allows, wrap the pastry in plastic wrap and chill in the fridge for 30 minutes.

Preheat the oven to 180°C/350°F/gas mark 4. Roll the pastry out until it is large enough to cover the base of the tin and trim the edges neatly.

To make the topping, place the chocolate, sugar, golden syrup and butter in a saucepan over a low heat, stirring occasionally until melted. Leave the mixture to cool a little and then stir in the eggs and pecans. Pour over the pastry and bake for 25–30 minutes, until set.

Leave to cool in the tin and then cut into bars. Store the bars in an airtight container.

Sticky Fruit and Whisky Slice

Makes 16
Preparation time: 1 hour, plus several hours soaking
You will need a Swiss roll tin measuring
23 x 30 cm/9 x 12 inches

Pastry
175 g/6 oz butter
50 g/1¾ oz caster sugar, plus extra for sprinkling
1 egg yolk
320 g/11 oz plain flour, sifted

Topping
200 g/7 oz muscovado sugar
200 g/7 oz butter
80 ml/3 fl oz whisky
4 eggs, beaten
200 g/7 oz currants
200 g/7 oz raisins
100 g/3½ oz glacé cherries, chopped
150 g/5 oz walnuts, chopped

This recipe is one of my absolute favourites. A lovely jumble of dried fruits and walnuts in a sticky, toffee-flavour topping, and it all comes with a kick of whisky too. I keep these in the freezer around Christmas time and defrost them for unexpected guests; they make a fabulous alternative to mince pies. Rustle up a tray of these, add a large jug of hot creamy custard and you have the perfect festive dessert.

To make the pastry, cream the butter and sugar together until light and smooth and then beat in the egg yolk. Add the flour and bring the mixture together to form a smooth pastry dough. Wrap the pastry in plastic wrap and chill in the fridge for 30 minutes.

Preheat the oven to 180°C/350°F/gas mark 4. Roll the pastry out to a size that is large enough to cover the base of the tin, then trim the edges neatly.

To make the topping, heat the sugar and butter together until the butter has melted and the sugar has dissolved. Stir in the whisky and leave the mixture to cool a little.

Add the eggs, and then stir in the currants, raisins, cherries and walnuts. Pour the mixture over the pastry base and bake for 30 minutes, or until the topping has set. Sprinkle the cake with caster sugar.

Allow to cool in the tin and then cut into bars. Store in an airtight container.

Variation:
Ring the changes by using different combinations of dried fruit – just take care to make sure that the total weight of the fruit remains the same. Candied orange peel adds a lovely flavour, in which case you might like to replace the whisky with an orange liqueur, such as Grand Marnier.

Zesty Apricot and Pecan Squares

Makes 15
Preparation time: 45 minutes, plus cooling
You will need a lightly buttered deep roasting tin
or cake tin measuring 20 x 30 cm/8 x 12 inches

100 g/3½ oz self-raising flour, sifted
100 g/3½ oz caster sugar
100 g/3½ oz desiccated coconut
150 g/5 oz dried apricots, chopped
100 g/3½ oz pecans, chopped
zest of 1 lime
200 g/7 oz butter, melted
2 eggs, beaten

Icing
300 g/10 oz icing sugar
30 g/1 oz butter, melted
1–2 tablespoons lime juice

Preheat the oven to 180°C/350°F/gas mark 4. Stir the
flour, sugar, coconut, apricots, pecans and lime zest together.
Add the melted butter and eggs and mix until thoroughly
combined. Spoon into the prepared tin and bake for
25 minutes or so, until golden and springy.

Remove from the oven and set aside to cool.

To make the icing, mix the icing sugar and butter with
the lime juice and spread evenly over the cooled cake.
Leave to set and then cut into squares or bars. Store in
an airtight container.

Sticky Coconut and Chocolate Bars

Makes 14
Preparation time: 40 minutes
You will need a well-buttered, shallow roasting pan or
cake tin measuring 20 x 30 cm/8 x 12 inches, ideally
lined with baking parchment

250 g/9 oz desiccated coconut
200 g/7 oz caster sugar
100 g/3½ oz butter, melted
2 eggs, lightly beaten
150 g/5 oz dark chocolate

The first time I made these delicious bars, I didn't
realise how important it would be to butter the tin
well. I couldn't wait to try them – I love the sweet
scent of coconut baking in the oven and the kitchen
that day smelled like a dream. But when it came to
cutting them, I couldn't prise the bars out of the tin.
So lots of butter on the tin here please – or a lining
of baking parchment, which is even better.

Preheat the oven to 180°C/350°F/gas mark 4. Mix the
coconut and sugar together in a large bowl. Stir in the butter
and then the eggs.

Press half of the mixture into the base of the prepared tin,
packing it down quite tightly and making sure that it forms
an even layer.

Roughly chop the chocolate and scatter this in an even
layer over the coconut base. Spread the remaining coconut
mixture over the chocolate and press down lightly.

Bake for about 20 minutes, until firm and golden. Remove
from the oven, and leave in the tin until completely cold.
Remove the baking parchment (if using), cut into bars and
then store in an airtight container.

Orange Blossom Honey and Sesame Bars

Makes 16
Preparation time: 1 hour and 10 minutes, plus
30 minutes resting for the pastry
You will need a Swiss roll pan measuring
23 x 32 cm/9 x 12 inches

Pastry
175 g/6 oz butter
50 g/1¾ oz caster sugar
1 egg yolk
320 g/11 oz plain flour, sifted

Topping
50 g/1¾ oz butter
400 g/14 oz clear orange blossom honey
85 g/3 oz golden caster sugar
200 g/7 oz fresh breadcrumbs
2 eggs
100 g/3½ oz sesame seeds
5 tablespoons mascarpone cheese

This is first cousin to treacle tart – the same chewy, gooey texture but with the flavour of orange blossom honey and the crunch of sesame seeds. It freezes beautifully, so is another recipe perfect for layering in greaseproof paper and storing in the freezer to defrost when needed. Try warming the bars in the oven and serving them as a dessert with some sliced bananas and fresh creamy custard. Sticky and sublime.

Cream the butter and sugar together until light and smooth and then beat in the egg yolk. Add the flour, and bring the mixture together to form a smooth dough. If time allows, wrap the pastry in plastic wrap and chill in the fridge for 30 minutes.

Preheat the oven to 190°C/370°C/gas mark 5. Roll the pastry out until it is large enough to cover the base of the tray, then trim the edges neatly.

Gently heat the butter, honey and caster sugar together in a small saucepan until the butter has melted and the sugar has dissolved (alternatively microwave on full power for 1 minute). Leave the mixture to cool a little, and then beat in the remaining ingredients. Pour the mixture over the pastry base and bake for 35–40 minutes, until the topping is golden and set.

Remove from the oven and allow to cool in the tin. Cut into bars and store in an airtight container.

Espresso Slices

Makes 25
Preparation time: 1¼ hours, plus 30 minutes resting
for the pastry
You will need a Swiss roll tin measuring
24 x 36 cm/9½ x 14 inches

Pastry
175 g/6 oz butter
50 g/1¾ oz caster sugar
1 egg yolk
320 g/11 oz plain flour, sifted

Filling
250 g/9 oz butter
500 g/1 lb 2 oz muscovado sugar
20 g/¾ oz finely ground espresso beans
150 ml/5 fl oz Kahlúa liqueur
4 eggs, lightly beaten
100 g/3½ oz self-raising flour, sifted

Decoration
40 g/1¾ oz dark chocolate
whole coffee beans

Made with dark sticky muscovado sugar, coffee and kahlua, they're perfect with morning coffee, but I love to serve them as petit fours too, cut into dainty pieces.

To make the pastry, cream the butter and sugar together until light and smooth and then beat in the egg yolk. Add the flour, and bring the mixture together to form a smooth pastry dough. If time allows, wrap the pastry in plastic wrap and chill in the fridge for 30 minutes.

Preheat the oven to 180°C/350°F/gas mark 4. Roll the pastry out until it is large enough to cover the base of the tin, then trim the edges neatly.

To make the filling, heat the butter and sugar together until melted. Add the sugar, ground beans and Kahlúa. Stir in the eggs and then lightly fold in the flour. Pour the mixture onto the pastry and bake for 25–30 minutes, until the topping has just set.

Remove from the oven and set aside to cool in the tin. Cut into slices.

Melt the chocolate in a bowl over a pan of hot water. Dip in the espresso beans to coat them. Leave to set, then arrange them on the slices. Store in an airtight container.

Something Fruity

Raspberry and White Chocolate Squares

Makes 15
Preparation time: 2 hours, including cooling and icing
You will need a lightly buttered, deep roasting pan or cake tin measuring 20 x 30 cm/8 x 12 inches

Cake
250 g/9 oz butter
250 g/9 oz caster sugar
4 eggs
250 g/9 oz self-raising flour
200 g/7 oz fresh raspberries

Topping
2 tablespoons caster sugar
150 g/5 oz white chocolate

Preheat the oven to 180°C/350°C/gas mark 4. Cream the butter and sugar together until light and fluffy. Add the eggs, a little at a time, stirring in between each addition, until the mixture is smooth and all the eggs are incorporated.

Add the flour and beat until smooth. Using a large metal spoon, carefully fold in the raspberries, taking care not to crush them too much. Spoon the mixture into the prepared tin and bake for 40 minutes, or until the cake is golden and springy. Leave to cool in the tin. Dust with caster sugar.

Melt the white chocolate in a bowl over a pan of simmering water (or alternatively, microwave on high for 1–2 minutes). Using the tip of a spoon or the tines of a fork, drizzle the white chocolate across the cooled caked using a backward and forward motion to create zigzagged lines. Leave to set and then cut into squares and store in an airtight container, in a cool place.

Cranberry, Apple and Almond Squares

Makes 15
Preparation time: 45 minutes
You will need a lightly buttered deep roasting tin or cake tin measuring 20 x 30 cm/8 x 12 inches

250 g/9 oz butter
250 g/9 oz caster sugar, plus extra for sprinkling
4 eggs, beaten
250 g/9 oz self-raising flour
150 g/5 oz dried cranberries
2 dessert apples, cored and chopped
150 g/5 oz flaked almonds

Preheat the oven to 180°C/350°F/gas mark 4. Cream the butter and sugar together until light and fluffy and then add the eggs, a little at a time until they are all fully incorporated. Stir in the flour, followed by the cranberries and apples. Add half of the almonds and then spoon the mixture into the prepared tin.
Scatter over the remaining almonds and bake for 30 minutes, or until golden and springy.

Leave to cool in the tin, sprinkle with a little caster sugar and cut into squares. Store in an airtight container.

Plum Cakes

Makes 15
Preparation time: 1 hour and 5 minutes
You will need a lightly buttered deep roasting tin
or cake tin measuring 20 x 30 cm/8 x 12 inches

250 g/9 oz butter
250 g/9 oz golden caster sugar
4 eggs, lightly beaten
300 g/10 oz self-raising flour
50 g/2 oz ground almonds
100 g/3½ oz fine polenta or semolina
1 teaspoon almond essence (optional)
500 g/1 lb 2 oz plums, halved and stones removed
caster sugar for sprinkling

Dotted with fresh plums and dusted with caster
sugar, these light-as-air squares of cake are pretty as
a picture. The darker skinned plum varieties such as
Friar and Sultan will add the lovely deep speckles that
you can see in the photograph opposite – although
other lighter varieties still have an excellent flavour.

Preheat the oven to 180°C/350°F/gas mark 4. Cream the
butter and sugar together until light and fluffy. Add the eggs,
a little at a time, until fully incorporated and the mixture is
smooth (if necessary, add a little of the flour to stop the
mixture curdling). Stir in the remaining flour, the ground
almonds, polenta or semolina, and almond essence, if using.

Place the plums in a food processor. Whizz until you have
a textured purée. Stir into the cake mixture and spoon into
the tin. Bake for 30–40 minutes, until golden brown and
risen and the cake springs back when touched in the centre
with the tip of the index finger.

Remove from the oven and set aside to cool. Sprinkle
with caster sugar and cut into squares. Store the cakes in
an airtight container.

Apricot and Oat Slices

Makes 15
Preparation time: 1 hour, plus cooling
You will need a baking tin measuring
24 x 36 cm/9½ x 14 inches

Filling
500 g/1 lb 2 oz dried apricots, chopped
100 g/3½ oz caster sugar

Crumble
250 g/9 oz butter
350 g/12 oz flour
200 g/7 oz caster sugar
50 g/1¾ oz jumbo oats

To make the filling, put the apricots and sugar in a saucepan with 100 ml/4 fl oz water. Simmer for 10–15 minutes, until the apricots are soft. Remove from the heat and leave to cool. Preheat the oven to 190°C/375°F/gas mark 5. Rub the butter and flour together until the mixture resembles coarse breadcrumbs. Add the sugar and oats.

Sprinkle half of the mixture over the base of the tin and press down gently. Spread the apricot mixture over the base. Scatter the remaining crumble evenly over the apricots. Bake for 25–30 minutes, until golden brown.

Remove from the oven and cut into squares or slices. Store in an airtight container.

Fig and Banana Lattice Bars

Makes 16
Preparation time: 1 hour, plus 30 minutes resting for the pastry
You will need a Swiss roll tin measuring
23 x 30 cm/9 x 12 inches

Pastry
250 g/9 oz butter
100 g/3½ oz caster sugar, plus extra for sprinkling
1 egg yolk
450 g/1 lb plain flour, sifted

Filling
600 g/1 lb 5 oz ready-to-eat dried figs, chopped
2 ripe bananas, sliced

To make the pastry, cream the butter and sugar together until they are light and smooth and then beat in the egg yolk. Add the flour, and bring the mixture together to form a smooth dough. If time allows, wrap the pastry in plastic wrap and chill in the fridge for 30 minutes.

To make the filling, put the figs in a saucepan with 150 ml/5 fl oz water. Cook over a medium heat for about 10 minutes, until the figs are very soft. Whizz briefly in a food processor, or mash well with a fork, until the figs form a smoothish paste. Add the bananas.

Preheat the oven to 180°C/350°F/gas mark 4. Lightly flour the work surface. Roll out slightly less than half the pastry and use to line the baking tin. Spread the fig mixture evenly over the pastry base.

Roll out the remaining pastry and cut it into long strips about 1 cm/½ inch wide. Use the strips to form a lattice pattern over the fig paste. Bake for 25–30 minutes, until the pastry is golden brown.

Remove from the oven and leave to cool. Sprinkle over a little caster sugar and cut into slices or bars. Store in an airtight container.

Apple and Blueberry Sweet Cheese Pastry Slices

Makes 15
Preparation time: 50 minutes, plus 30 minutes resting
for pastry
You will need a Swiss roll pan measuring
20 x 30 cm/8 x 12 inches

Pastry
200 g/7 oz butter
50 g/1¾ oz sugar
2 egg yolks
450 g/1 lb flour
150 g/5 oz Cheddar or Jack cheese

Filling
4–5 cooking apples
100 g/3½ oz caster sugar (or to taste),
   plus extra to sprinkle
100 g/3½ oz dried blueberries

1 egg white, lightly whisked

The combination of cheese and fruit might at first seem unusual, but the sweet-savoury partnership actually brings out the best of both flavours.

Cream the butter and sugar together until light and smooth, then beat in the egg yolks. Add the flour and cheese, and bring the mixture together to form a smooth dough. Wrap the pastry in plastic wrap and chill in the fridge for 30 minutes.

Place the apples and sugar together in a saucepan with 4–5 tablespoons of water and cook for 10–15 minutes until softened. Stir in the blueberries and check for sweetness, adding a little more sugar if necessary. Leave to cool.

Preheat the oven to 180°C/350°C/gas mark 4. Scatter a work surface with flour, roll out half of the pastry and use it to line the baking tray.

Spread the apple mixture over the pastry. Roll out the remaining pastry and lay it over the apples. Brush the pastry with egg white and scatter with caster sugar.

Bake for 30–35 minutes, until golden. Leave to cool and cut into squares or slices.

Raspberry and Mascarpone Shortbread

Makes 24
Preparation time: 50 minutes
You will need a Swiss roll tin measuring
27 x 30 cm/11 x 12 inches

125 g/4½ oz fine polenta
250 g/9 oz plain flour
125 g/4½ oz caster sugar
250 g/9 oz butter
500 g/1 lb 2 oz mascarpone
150 g/5 oz caster sugar, plus extra for sprinkling
750 g/1 lb 10 oz raspberries

This is a big bake for a big occasion; in fact ideal as a finale for a barbecue party or such. The great thing is that it's so easy and so versatile; you can run with the seasons. Here I've used raspberries to top the layer of sweet polenta shortbread – but strawberries, blackberries or blueberries (in fact any type of sweet berry) all work well. Stone fruits are superb – from sliced summer peaches to ripe autumn plums. Even chunks of dessert apples or pears sautéed in a little butter are incredibly delicious.

Preheat the oven to 180°C/350°F/gas mark 4. Combine the polenta, flour and sugar together in a bowl and then rub in the butter until the mixture resembles breadcrumbs. Squeeze the mixture together to form a dough and press it into the prepared tin. Bake for 25 minutes or so, until golden and firm. Leave to cool.

Beat the mascarpone with the sugar until light and fluffy. Spread over the cooled shortbread base. Arrange the raspberries over the top and scatter with a little extra caster sugar. Cut into squares or bars and store in the fridge.

Variation:
Try this apple and raisin topping as an autumn alternative to raspberries.

8–10 crisp dessert apples
100 g/3½ oz butter
caster sugar, to taste
150 g/5 oz raisins
50 ml/2 fl oz Calvados

Core the apples (but leave the skin on) and cut them into dice. Heat the butter in a large frying pan or saucepan and add the apples. Cook for 4–5 minutes until they start to soften and then add sugar to taste (the amount will vary according to the apple variety you are using and their degree of natural sweetness). Add the raisins and cook for another 2–3 minutes. Finally, add the Calvados and carefully flame.

Leave to cool, trying hard not to eat the mixture while you wait. When completely cold, spread the mixture over the mascarpone and cut into squares or bars. Store in the fridge.

Apple and Cinnamon Slices

Makes 15
Preparation time: 50 minutes, plus cooling
You will need a Swiss roll tin measuring
23 x 30 cm/9 x 12 inches

Pastry
350 g/12 oz butter
100 g/3½ oz caster sugar
2 egg yolks
600 g/1 lb 5 oz plain flour, sifted

Filling
4–5 cooking apples, cored and chopped
100 g/3½ oz caster sugar, or to taste
1 teaspoon ground cinnamon
100 g/3½ oz sultanas

1 egg white, lightly whisked
2–3 tablespoons caster sugar, for sprinkling

To make the filling, place the apples and sugar in a saucepan
with 4–5 tablespoons of water and cook for 10–15 minutes
until softened. Stir in the sultanas and check for sweetness,
adding a little more sugar if necessary. Leave to cool.

Meanwhile, make the pastry by creaming the butter and
sugar together until light and smooth and then beating in the
egg yolks. Add the flour, and bring the mixture together to
form a smooth pastry dough. If time allows, wrap the pastry
in plastic wrap and chill in the fridge for 30 minutes.

Preheat the oven to 180°C/350°F/gas mark 4. Lightly
flour a work surface and roll out half of the pastry to use to
line the baking tin. Spread the apples over the pastry base.

Roll out the remaining pastry and lay it carefully over the
apples. Brush the pastry with egg white and sprinkle with
caster sugar. Bake for 40 minutes or so, until golden.

Leave to cool and cut into squares or slices. Store in an
airtight container.

Spiced Pear Slices

Makes 15
Preparation time: 1 hour and 10 minutes, plus freezing
time for the pastry
You will need a Swiss roll tin measuring
23 x 30 cm/9 x 12 inches

Pastry
175 g/6 oz butter
50 g/1¾ oz caster sugar
1 egg yolk
320 g/11 oz plain flour, sifted

Filling
50 g/1¾ oz butter
1 kg/2 lb 2 oz firm but ripe pears, cored and diced
100 g/3½ oz caster sugar
1 teaspoon finely ground star anise

To make the filling, melt the butter in a saucepan. Add the
pears and fry until soft and golden. Stir in the sugar and star
anise and cook for a further 2–3 minutes. Leave to cool.

Meanwhile, make the pastry by creaming the butter and
sugar together until light and smooth and then beat in the
egg yolk. Add the flour, and bring the mixture together to
form a smooth pastry dough. Place half the pastry in the
freezer until firm enough to grate. Wrap the remaining pastry
in plastic wrap and chill in the fridge for 30 minutes.

Preheat the oven to 180°C/350°F/gas mark 4. Roll the
chilled pastry out until it is large enough to cover the base
of the tin and trim the edges neatly. Spread the pear mixture
evenly over the pastry base.

Grate the remaining pastry and scatter over the pears.
Bake for 25 minutes, until golden brown.

Cool and cut into slices. Store in an airtight container.

Apricot and Coconut Squares

Makes 15
Preparation time: 45 minutes
You will need a lightly buttered deep roasting tin or
cake tin measuring 20 x 30 cm/8 x 12 inches

Base
100 g/3½ oz self-raising flour
100 g/3½ oz desiccated coconut
100 g/3½ oz caster sugar
100 g/3½ oz butter, melted

Topping
200 g/7 oz dried apricots, chopped
150 g/5oz caster sugar
50 g/1¾ oz desiccated coconut
100 g/3½ oz walnuts, roughly chopped
2 eggs, beaten

50 g/1¾ oz dark chocolate, melted

Preheat the oven to 180°C/350°F/gas mark 4. To make the
base, sift the flour into a bowl and add the coconut and
caster sugar. Stir in the melted butter and spoon the mixture
into the prepared tin.

To make the topping, mix the apricots, sugar, coconut and
walnuts together in a large bowl and stir in the eggs. Spread
over the base and then bake for 20–25 minutes, until golden
and springy. Leave to cool.

Drizzle the cold cake with the melted chocolate to
decorate and then cut into squares or bars. Store them in
an airtight container.

Apple and Sultana Squares

Makes 15
Preparation time: 45 minutes
You will need a lightly buttered deep roasting tin
or cake tin measuring 20 x 30 cm/8 x 12 inches

250 g/9 oz butter
250 g/9 oz caster sugar, plus extra for sprinkling
4 eggs, beaten
250 g/9 oz self-raising flour
2 tart dessert apples, cored and coarsely chopped
100 g/3½ oz sultanas

Preheat the oven to 180°C/350°F/gas mark 4. Cream the
butter and sugar together until light and fluffy and then add
the eggs, a little at a time until they are all fully incorporated.
Fold in the flour. Stir in the apples and sultanas. Spoon the
mixture into the prepared tin and bake for 25 minutes,
until golden and springy.

Leave to cool in the tin and then sprinkle with caster sugar
and cut into squares. Store in an airtight container.

Carrot Cakes

Makes 15
Preparation time: 1¼ hours, plus cooling
You will need a lightly buttered deep roasting tin or
cake tin measuring 20 x 30 cm/8 x 12 inches

250 g/9 oz butter
250 g/9 oz golden caster sugar
4 eggs, beaten
300 g/10 oz self-raising flour, sifted
2 large carrots, peeled and grated
2 teaspoons ground cinnamon
juice and zest 1 orange
50 g/1¾ oz sultanas

Topping
250 g/9 oz mascarpone
100 g/3½ oz caster sugar, plus extra for sprinkling
zest 2 oranges

Moist and fruity, this freezes well and so is another recipe that can be defrosted to order. The mascarpone topping makes a brilliant alternative to the customary cream cheese topping that accompanies many carrot cakes. If you are going to freeze some, however, it is a good idea to do so before adding the mascarpone – simply add a swirl once the cakes are defrosted and they are ready to serve.

Preheat the oven to 180°C/350°F/gas mark 4. Cream the butter and sugar together until pale and fluffy and then beat in the eggs, a little at a time until the mixture is smooth, adding a little flour in between each addition to prevent curdling. Stir in the remaining flour, the grated carrot, the cinnamon and orange juice and zest, retaining a sprinkling of zest to decorate the finished cakes. Add the sultanas. Spoon the mixture into the prepared tin and bake for 50 minutes, or until risen and golden. Cool in the tin.

To make the topping, beat the mascarpone and sugar together. Cut the cake into squares and decorate with little dollops of the mascarpone mixture and a piece of orange zest sprinkled with a little caster sugar.

Banana and Pecan Squares

Makes 15
Preparation time: 45 minutes
You will need a lightly buttered deep roasting tin
or cake tin measuring 20 x 30 cm/8 x 12 inches

200 g/7 oz butter
200 g/7 oz caster sugar
3 eggs, beaten
200 g/7 oz self-raising flour
2 ripe bananas, mashed
150 g/5oz pecan nuts, roughly chopped
demerara sugar, for sprinkling

Preheat the oven to 180°C/350°F/gas mark 4. Cream the
butter and sugar together until light and fluffy and then add
the eggs, a little at a time until they are all fully incorporated.
Fold in the flour.

Stir in the mashed bananas and the pecans. Spoon into
the prepared tin and bake for 25 minutes until the cake is
golden and springy.

Leave to cool in the tin and then dust with demerara sugar
and cut into squares. Store in an airtight container.

Blueberry and Hazelnut Bars

Makes 15
Preparation time: 1 hour and 10 minutes, plus
30 minutes resting for pastry
You will need a lightly buttered deep roasting tin
or cake tin measuring 20 x 30 cm/8 x 12 inches

250 g/9 oz butter
250 g/9 oz caster sugar
4 eggs, beaten
250 g/9 oz self-raising flour

Topping
300 g/10 oz dried blueberries
100 g/3½ oz demerara sugar
100 g/3½ oz chopped hazelnuts, roasted
50 g/1¾ oz butter, melted
zest 1 lemon

Preheat the oven to 180°C/350°F/gas mark 4. Cream the
butter and sugar together until light and fluffy and then add
the eggs, a little at a time until they are all fully incorporated.
Fold in the flour. Spoon into the prepared tin.

To make the topping, combine the blueberries, sugar and
hazelnuts. Stir in the melted butter and lemon zest. Spoon
evenly over the cake batter in the tin. Bake for 30 minutes
or so, until golden and springy.

Leave to cool in the tin and then cut into squares or bars.
Store in an airtight container.

Pear and Polenta Slices

Makes 15
Preparation time: 1¼ hours
You will need a Swiss roll tin measuring
24 x 28 cm/9¾ x 11 inches

200 g/7 oz ground almonds
350 g/12 oz plain flour
200 g/7 oz polenta
250 g/9 oz caster sugar, plus 1 tablespoon for sprinkling
250 g/9 oz butter
2 teaspoons ground cinnamon
4 egg yolks
4 ripe but firm pears
juice ½ lemon

Preheat the oven to 180°C/350°F/gas mark 4. Place the almonds, flour, polenta and sugar in a large bowl and rub in the butter until the mixture resembles coarse breadcrumbs. Stir in the cinnamon and then the egg yolks. The mixture should now have a sticky texture – not quite crumble, not quite pastry.

Grate the pears into a bowl and stir in the lemon juice. Press half of the crumbly mixture over the baking tin and press down firmly. Scatter the pears evenly over and then sprinkle the remaining crumble mixture over the top. Bake for 50 minutes or so, until golden and crisp.

Leave to cool, then sprinkle with a little caster sugar and cut into squares. Store in an airtight container.

Crumbly Date Slices

Makes 15
Preparation time: 1 hour
You will need a Swiss roll tin measuring
23 x 30 cm/9 x 12 inches

Filling
600 g/1 lb 5 oz dates, pitted and roughly chopped
  (or substitute chopped sugar-rolled dates)
100 g/3½ oz light muscovado sugar (omit the sugar if
  using sugar-rolled dates)

Crumble
350 g/12 oz plain flour
250 g/9 oz butter
200 g/7 oz light muscovado sugar
50 g/1¾ oz walnuts, coarsely chopped

To make the filling, put the dates and sugar (unless using sugar-rolled dates) in a saucepan with 100 ml/4 fl oz water and simmer for 10 minutes or so, until the dates are soft. Remove from the heat and leave to cool.

Preheat the oven to 190°C/375°F/gas mark 5. To make the crumble, rub the flour and butter together until the mixture resembles coarse breadcrumbs. Add the sugar and walnuts. Sprinkle half over the base of the tin and press down gently. Spread the date mixture over the base. Scatter the remaining crumble evenly over the dates. Bake for 25–30 minutes, until the crumble is golden brown.

Remove from the oven and cut into squares or slices. Store in an airtight container.

Orange Marmalade and Chestnut Brownies

Makes 15
Preparation time: 1 hour
You will need a lightly buttered roasting pan or cake tin measuring 20 x 30 cm/8 x 10 inches

250 g/9 oz butter
500 g/1 lb 2 oz caster sugar
100 g/3½ oz dark chocolate
50 g/1¾ oz cocoa powder
4 eggs, beaten
100 g/3½ oz self-raising flour
4 tablespoons orange marmalade
100 g/3½ oz cooked and peeled chestnuts (I use canned)
    coarsely chopped

Marmalade adds a lovely flavour to brownies. I've used ginger marmalade on occasions too and been pleased with the results. If you're not keen on chestnuts, then roughly chopped hazelnuts make a great alternative.

Preheat the oven to 180°C/350°F/gas mark 4. Melt the butter, sugar, chocolate and cocoa powder together. Stir in the beaten eggs and fold in the flour. Stir in the marmalade and the chestnuts.

Spoon the mixture into the prepared tin and bake for 35 minutes, or until firm but fudgy. Cool in the tin and then cut into squares. Store in an airtight container.

Spiced Pumpkin Squares

Makes 15
Preparation time: 1 hour and 10 minutes
You will need a lightly buttered deep roasting tin or cake tin measuring 20 x 30 cm/8 x 12 inches

300 g/10 oz plain flour
1 teaspoon bicarbonate of soda
1 teaspoon ground ginger
1 teaspoon ground cinnamon
200 g/7 oz muscovado sugar
150 ml/5 fl oz golden syrup
150 g/5 oz pumpkin purée (canned is fine)
100 g/3½ oz butter, melted
2 eggs, beaten
150 g/5 oz crystallized ginger, roughly chopped

The idea of adding pumpkin to the mix may seem a little strange, but it adds a delightful moistness and flavour that marries so well with the dark sugar and spices. Dark and dense and dotted with little nuggets of crystallized ginger, this cake benefits from being wrapped up and tucked away in a tin for a few days.

Preheat the oven to 180°C/350°F/gas mark 4. Sift the flour and bicarbonate of soda together into a large bowl. Add the spices and sugar.

In a separate bowl, whisk together the golden syrup, the pumpkin purée, melted butter and eggs. Pour into the dry ingredients and beat until smooth. Stir in the ginger. Pour into the prepared tin and bake for 45–50 minutes until the cake is risen and springy.

Leave to cool in the tin and then cut into squares or bars. Store in an airtight container.

Something
Special

Lemon Poppy Seed Bars

Makes 15

Preparation time: 1 hour and 20 minutes, plus cooling

You will need a lightly buttered deep roasting tin or cake tin measuring 20 x 30 cm/8 x 12 inches

250 g/9 oz butter
250 g/9 oz caster sugar
4 eggs
250 g/9 oz self-raising flour
zest and juice 1 lemon
100 g/3½ oz poppy seeds

Icing
300 g/10 oz icing sugar
zest and juice 1 large lemon
3–4 tablespoons lemon curd

These bars are cloaked in a generous layer of lemon icing that has a feathering of lemon curd through it too. When you drag the skewer through the lemon curd, make sure that the icing is still wet, or the feathering won't be as effective or attractive.

Preheat the oven to 180°C/350°F/gas mark 4. Cream the butter and sugar together until light and fluffy. Add the eggs, a little at a time, stirring in between each addition, until the mixture is smooth and all the eggs have been incorporated. Stir in the flour, and then beat in the lemon zest and juice, and the poppy seeds. Spoon into the prepared tin and bake for 30–35 minutes, until golden and springy to the touch.

Remove from the oven and leave to cool in the tin.

To make the icing, sift the icing sugar into a large bowl and add the lemon zest and enough of the lemon juice to make a consistency similar to thick pouring cream. Pour the icing over the cold cake and spread carefully with a palette knife. Leave until almost set and then pipe thin rows of lemon curd at equal distances across the cakes. Drag the point of a skewer through the lemon curd at a 90° angle to form a feathered pattern, and then leave to set. Cut into bars and store in an airtight container.

Crunchy Rum Bars

Makes 15
Preparation time: 40 minutes, plus 1½ hours setting
You will need a lightly buttered deep roasting tin or cake tin measuring 20 x 30 cm/8 x 12 inches

500 g/1 lb 2oz chocolate digestives, crushed
100 g/3½ oz desiccated coconut
200 g/7 oz pecan nuts, roughly chopped
200 g/7 oz raisins
250 g/9 oz dark chocolate
150 g/5 oz butter
50 g/1¾ oz cocoa powder
2 tablespoons golden syrup
3 tablespoons dark rum
2 eggs, beaten

Icing
200 g/7 oz dark chocolate
100 g/3½ oz butter
1 tablespoon dark rum

Place the biscuits, coconut, pecans and raisins in a large bowl. Melt the chocolate, butter, cocoa powder and golden syrup together. Stir in the rum, and then stir this into the dry ingredients. Stir in the eggs and spoon the mixture into the prepared tin. Leave to set in the fridge for an hour or so.

To make the icing, melt the chocolate and beat in the butter and rum. Continue beating until the mixture is thick and glossy. Leave to cool and then spread over the rum cake. Return to the refrigerator for 30 minutes, or until the topping has set. Cut into squares or bars and store in an airtight container in the fridge.

White Chocolate and Almond Brownies

Makes 15
Preparation time: 1¼ hours
You will need a lightly buttered roasting tin or cake tin measuring 20 x 30 cm/8 x 12 inches

200 g/7 oz white chocolate, chopped
175 g/6 oz butter
400 g/14 oz icing sugar
4 eggs
100 g/3½ oz ground almonds
85 g/3 oz self-raising flour
100 g/3½ oz pecans, roughly chopped

Preheat the oven to 180°C/350°F/gas mark 4. Melt the chocolate, butter and sugar in a saucepan over a gentle heat. Stir until smooth, remove from the heat and set aside to cool slightly.

Stir the eggs into the chocolate mixture, and then fold in the ground almonds and flour. Stir in the pecans. Spoon into the prepared tin and bake for 40–50 minutes, until just firm but still slightly fudgy.

Cool in the tin and then cut into squares. Store them in an airtight container.

Dark Chocolate and Almond Squares

Makes 15
Preparation time: 1½ hours
You will need a lightly buttered deep roasting tin
or cake tin measuring 20 x 30 cm/8 x 12 inches

400 g/14 oz dark chocolate
8 eggs, separated
400 g/14 oz caster sugar
500 g/1 lb 2 oz ground almonds
400 g/14 oz butter, melted
3 tablespoons rum
icing sugar, for dusting

Preheat the oven to 180°C/350°F/gas mark 4. Break the
chocolate into a food processor and blitz until the chocolate
has the texture of course crumbs.

Whisk the egg yolks and sugar together until thick, pale
and light. Fold in the ground almonds and the chocolate,
trickle in the butter and stir gently until evenly incorporated.
Stir in the rum.

In a separate bowl, whisk the egg whites until they form
peaks. Fold into the chocolate mixture. Spoon into the
prepared tin and bake for 1 hour, until springy to the touch.

Leave to cool in the tin, dust with icing sugar, and then
cut into squares. Store in an airtight container.

Florentine Slices

Makes 24
Preparation time: 45 minutes, plus 30 minutes setting
You will need a lightly buttered Swiss roll tin
measuring 27 x 30 cm/11 x 12 inches

200 g/7 oz cornflakes, roughly crushed
250 g/9 oz mixed glacé pineapple, mango and papaya
150 g/5 oz glacé cherries
50 g/1¾ oz crystallized ginger
50 g/1¾ oz sultanas
50 g/1¾ oz flaked almonds
375 ml/13 fl oz can condensed milk
100 g/3½ oz white chocolate

Preheat the oven to 180°C/350°F/gas mark 4. Put the
cornflakes in a large bowl with the fruit and almonds. Stir in
the condensed milk.

Spoon into the prepared tin and bake for 10–15 minutes,
until golden and set.

Mark into bars while still slightly warm and then cut
through when completely cold.

Melt the white chocolate in a bowl over a saucepan of
gently simmering water. Stir until smooth. Drizzle over the
bars and store in the fridge.

Iced Crystallized Ginger Squares

Makes 15
Preparation time: 1½ hours, plus cooling
You will need a lightly buttered deep roasting tin or
cake tin measuring 20 x 30 cm/8 x 12 inches

320 g/11 oz plain flour
2 tablespoons bicarbonate of soda
2 teaspoons ground ginger
2 teaspoons ground cinnamon
180g/6½ oz butter
100 ml/4 fl oz milk
250 ml/9 fl oz soured cream
2 eggs
400 g/14 oz muscovado sugar
6 pieces crystallized ginger, roughly chopped
100 g/3½ oz sultanas

Icing
300 g/10 oz icing sugar
zest and juice 1–2 lemons
15 pieces crystallized ginger, to decorate

Crystallized ginger has a sweet spicy flavour that
is ideally suited to baking. The lemon icing tastes
delicous against the ground ginger and cinnamon
in the sponge cake.

Preheat the oven to 180°C/350°F/gas mark 4. Sift the
flour, bicarbonate of soda and spices into a large bowl.
  Place the butter and milk in a saucepan and heat gently
until the butter has melted. Pour into the flour mixture
and stir well until thoroughly combined. Add the soured
cream and eggs, and then stir in the sugar, ginger and
sultanas. Spoon the mixture into the prepared tin and
bake for 50 minutes or so, until firm but springy.
  Leave to cool in the tin, then cut it into squares.
  To make the icing, mix the icing sugar, lemon zest and
enough lemon juice to give a thick pouring consistency, and
carefully ice the cakes. Decorate each one with a piece of
cystallized ginger. Store in an airtight container.

Almond and Chocolate Fudge Squares

Makes 15
Preparation time: 1 hour, plus cooling
You will need a lightly buttered deep roasting tin or cake tin measuring 20 x 30 cm/8 x 12 inches

250 g/9 oz butter
350 g/12 oz caster sugar
6 eggs, beaten
150 g/5 oz plain flour
150 g/5 oz ground almonds
1 teaspoon almond essence

Fudge topping
180 g/6¼ oz sugar
100 g/3½ oz butter
250 g/9 oz dark chocolate
150 ml/5 fl oz evaporated milk

Preheat the oven to 180°C/350°F/gas mark 4. Cream the butter and sugar together until pale and fluffy and then beat in the eggs, a little at a time until the mixture is smooth. You may have to add a little flour in between each addition to prevent curdling. Stir in the remaining flour, the ground almonds and almond essence. Spoon into the prepared tin and bake for 50 minutes or so, until risen and golden. Cool in the tin.

Meanwhile, make the fudge topping by placing all the ingredients in a saucepan and heating gently until the sugar has dissolved and the butter and chocolate have melted. Simmer over a low heat for 3–4 minutes, until the mixture thickens. Beat for 2–3 minutes until glossy and then refrigerate until cold.

Spread the topping over the cold cake. Cut into squares and store in an airtight container in a cool place.

Caribbean Rum and Spice Bars

Makes 16
Preparation time: 2 hours, plus 2–3 hours soaking
You will need a lightly buttered deep roasting tin or cake tin measuring 20 x 30 cm/8 x 12 inches

500 g/1 lb 2 oz mixed dried fruit, including raisins, cherries, chopped dates, chopped apricots
85 ml/3 fl oz dark rum, plus 4–5 tablespoons for drizzling
300 g/10 oz plain flour
2 teaspoons baking powder
2 teaspoons mixed spice
½ teaspoon grated nutmeg
250 g/9 oz butter
250 g/9 oz dark molasses sugar
4 eggs, beaten
100 g/3½ oz ground almonds
50 g/1¾ oz flaked almonds

Soak the fruit in the rum for at least 2–3 hours, or even overnight if possible.

Preheat the oven to 150°C/300°F/gas mark 2. Sift the flour, baking powder and spices together and set aside.

Beat the butter with the sugar until light and fluffy. Add the eggs, a little at a time, stirring. You may have to add a little flour in between each addition to prevent curdling. Stir in the remaining flour and the ground and flaked almonds. Then add the fruit and soaking liquid. Spoon into the prepared tin and bake for 1¼ hours or so, until a skewer inserted into the centre comes out clean.

Leave to cool in the tin and cut into bars. Store in an airtight container.

Lemon Yogurt Cake

Makes 15
Preparation time: 1 hour and 10 minutes
You will need a lightly buttered deep roasting tin or cake tin measuring 20 x 30 cm/8 x 12 inches

250 g/9 oz butter
250 g/9 oz caster sugar, plus extra for sprinkling
4 eggs, beaten
250 g/9 oz semolina
250 g/9 oz ground almonds
50 g/1¾ oz plain flour
2 teaspoons baking powder
zest and juice of 1 lemon
125 g/4½ oz natural yogurt
150 g/5 oz pine nuts

Syrup
juice of 4 lemons
200 g/7 oz caster sugar

Preheat the oven to 180°C/350°F/gas mark 4. Beat the butter and sugar together until pale and fluffy. Add the eggs, a little at a time, until fully incorporated. Stir in the semolina and ground almonds. Sift the flour and baking powder into the mixture and stir until thoroughly combined. Stir in the lemon juice and zest. Fold in the yogurt and half of the pine nuts. Spoon into the prepared tin and scatter over the remaining pine nuts. Bake for 35–40 minutes or so, until golden and springy.

To make the syrup, stir the lemon juice and caster sugar together. Remove the cake from the oven and immediately pour the lemon syrup evenly over the top of the cake; it will be absorbed as the cake cools. Sprinkle with a little caster sugar and cut into squares. Store in an airtight container.

Cardamom and Orange Brownies

Makes 15
Preparation time: 1 hour and 30 minutes, including soaking
You will need a lightly buttered roasting tin or cake tin measuring 20 x 30 cm/8 x 12 inches

250 g/9 oz butter
500 g/1 lb 2 oz caster sugar
100 g/3½ oz dark chocolate
50 g/1¾ oz cocoa powder
4 eggs, beaten
scant teaspoon cardamom seeds, crushed
zest 1 orange
100 g/3½ oz self-raising flour

Preheat the oven to 180°C/350°F/gas mark 4. Melt the butter, sugar, 50 g/1¾ oz of the chocolate, and the cocoa powder together in a pan set over a low heat. Remove from the heat and leave to cool slightly.

Stir the eggs into the chocolate mixture and then add the cardamom seeds and orange zest. Fold in the flour. Roughly chop the remaining chocolate and stir into the cocoa mixture. Spoon into the prepared tin, and then bake for 35 minutes or so, until just firm but still slightly fudgy.

Leave to cool in the tin and then cut into squares. Store in an airtight container.

Chocolate and Chestnut Bars

Makes 15
Preparation time: 1 hour and 10 minutes,
plus 30 minutes resting for the pastry
You will need a Swiss roll tin measuring
20 x 30 cm/10 x 12 inches

Pastry
175 g/6 oz butter
50 g/1¾ oz caster sugar
1 egg yolk
320 g/11 oz plain flour, sifted
450 g/1 lb apricot jam

Topping
400 g/14 oz cooked chestnuts
400 g/14 oz caster sugar
200 g/7 oz plain chocolate, melted
200 g/7 oz butter, melted
4 eggs

Icing
200 g/7 oz icing sugar
2–3 tablespoons Kahlúa

Cream the butter and sugar together until light and smooth
and then beat in the egg yolk. Add the flour, and bring the
mixture together to form a smooth dough. Wrap the pastry
in plastic wrap and chill in the fridge for 30 minutes.

Preheat the oven to 180°C/350°F/gas mark 4. Roll the
pastry out to cover the base of the tray and trim the edges
neatly. Spread the jam evenly over the pastry.

Put the chestnuts in a food processor and whizz until
finely ground. Transfer them to a large bowl and add the
sugar, chocolate, butter and eggs, and beat until smooth.
Spread the mixture evenly over the jam. Bake for 35 minutes,
or until firm. Set aside to cool in the tin.

Mix the icing sugar and Kahlúa together until the mixture
forms a smooth icing, adding a little water if necessary.
Drizzle over the cooled cake using a zigzag motion. Leave to
set. Cut into bars and store in an airtight container.

Coconut and Passion Fruit Slices

Makes 25
Preparation time: 1 hour and 20 minutes, plus
30 minutes resting for the pastry
You will need a Swiss roll tin measuring
24 x 36 cm/9¾ x 14 inches

Pastry
175 g/6 oz butter
50 g/1¾ oz caster sugar
1 egg yolk
320 g/11 oz plain flour, sifted
4–5 tablespoons orange curd

Topping
6 passion fruit, halved
4 eggs, beaten
600 ml/1 pint double cream
400 g/14 oz desiccated coconut
400 g/14 oz caster sugar
100 g/3½ oz plain flour
zest and juice of 1 lemon
zest and juice of 1 large orange

To make the pastry, cream the butter and sugar together
until light and smooth and then beat in the egg yolk.
Add the flour, and bring the mixture together to form a
smooth pastry dough. If time allows, wrap the pastry in
plastic wrap and chill in the fridge for 30 minutes.

Preheat the oven to 180°C/350°F/gas mark 4. Roll the
pastry out to cover the base of the tin and trim the edges
neatly. Spread the orange curd evenly over the pastry base.

To make the filling, remove the pulp from the passion
fruit and place into a bowl. Stir in the eggs and double
cream. Add the coconut and sugar and then beat in the flour.
Stir in the lemon and orange zests and juice. Pour over the
base and bake for 30 minutes or so, until golden and springy.

Set aside to cool in the tin and cut into bars. Store in an
airtight container.

Cherry, Chocolate and Kahlúa Brownies

Makes 15
Preparation time: 1 hour, plus 30 minutes soaking
You will need a lightly buttered roasting tin or cake tin measuring 20 x 30 cm/8 x 12 inches

100 g/3½ oz dried cherries
4–5 tablespoons Kahlúa
250 g/9 oz butter
500 g/1 lb 2 oz caster sugar
100 g/3½ oz dark chocolate
60 g/2¼ oz cocoa powder
4 eggs, beaten
125 g/4½ oz self-raising flour

Soak the cherries in the Kahlúa for 30 minutes or so.

Preheat the oven to 180°C/350°F/gas mark 4. Melt the butter, sugar, chocolate and cocoa powder together. Remove from the heat and leave to cool slightly.

Stir the eggs into the chocolate mixture and then fold in the flour. Stir in the cherries and soaking liquid. Spoon into the prepared tin, and then bake for 35 minutes or so, until just firm but still slightly fudgy.

Leave to cool in the tin and then cut into squares. Store them in an airtight container.

Butterscotch Cake

Makes 15
Preparation time: 40 minutes, plus cooling
You will need a lightly buttered deep roasting tin or cake tin measuring 20 x 30 cm/8 x 12 inches

250 g/9 oz butter
250 g/9 oz light muscovado sugar
4 eggs, beaten
250 g/9 oz self-raising flour

Icing
150 g/5 oz light muscovado sugar
150 g/5 oz icing sugar
150 g/5 oz butter, softened
100 g/3½ oz honeycomb candy, crushed
50 g/1¾ oz pecan nuts, roughly chopped

Preheat the oven to 180°C/350°F/gas mark 4. Cream the butter and sugar together until light and fluffy and then add the eggs, a little at a time until they are all fully incorporated. Stir in the flour. Spoon into the prepared tin and bake for 30 minutes or so, until golden and springy.

Leave to cool in the tin.

To make the icing, beat the sugars with the butter and spread over the cooled cake. Mix the crushed honeycomb with the pecans and scatter over the cake. Cut into squares and store in an airtight container.

Chewy Whisky, Date and Pistachio Bars

Makes 16
Preparation time: 1 hour and 10 minutes
You will need a lightly buttered deep roasting tin or cake tin measuring 20 x 30 cm/8 x 12 inches

100 g/3½ oz self-raising flour, sifted
100 g/3½ oz caster sugar
50 g/1¾ oz desiccated coconut
150 g/5oz chopped dates
100 g/3½ oz pistachio nuts
175 g/6 oz butter, melted
1 egg, beaten
3–4 tablespoons whisky

Topping
300 g/10 oz icing sugar
30 g/1 oz butter, melted
zest and juice ½ lemon

Preheat the oven to 180°C/350°F/gas mark 4. Stir the flour, sugar, coconut, dates and pistachios together in a large bowl. Add the melted butter and beaten egg and mix until they are thoroughly combined. Spoon into the prepared tin and bake for 25 minutes or so, until golden and springy. Sprinkle the whisky evenly over the warm cake and then leave to cool.

To make the topping, mix the icing sugar, butter and lemon juice and zest together and spread evenly over the cooled cake. Leave to set and then cut into squares or bars. Store them in an airtight container.

Lemon Cheesecake Brownies

Makes 15
Preparation time: 1½ hours
You will need a lightly buttered roasting tin or cake tin measuring 20 x 30 cm/8 x 12 inches

250 g/9 oz butter
500 g/1 lb 2 oz caster sugar
100 g/3½ oz cocoa powder
4 eggs, beaten
100 g/3½ oz self-raising flour

Cheesecake layer
500 g/1 lb 2 oz ricotta cheese
zest 1 lemon
4 egg yolks
100 g/3½ oz icing sugar

Preheat the oven to 180°C/350°F/gas mark 4. Melt the butter, sugar and cocoa powder together. Remove from the heat and leave to cool slightly.

Stir the eggs into the cocoa mixture, and then fold in the flour. Spoon into the prepared tin.

To make the cheesecake layer, beat the ricotta, lemon zest, egg yolks and icing sugar together until smooth, and then carefully drizzle randomly over the chocolate mixture. Bake for about 35 minutes, until just firm but still slightly fudgy.

Leave to cool in the tin and then cut into squares. Store in an airtight container.

Fruity Crumble Slices

Makes 15
Preparation time: 50 minutes
You will need a Swiss roll tin measuring
23 x 30 cm/9 x 12 inches

Filling
500 g/1 lb 2 oz mixed dried fruit, including glacé cherries,
　currants, raisins and sultanas
100 g/3½ oz muscovado sugar
100 g/3½ oz butter

Crumble
250 g/9 oz butter
400 g/14 oz flour
200 g/7 oz caster sugar
150 g/5 oz flaked almonds

These make a wonderful autumn or winter dessert.
Serve with a jug of steamy creamy custard, or a
brandy sauce with the faintest hint of nutmeg.

To make the filling, place the mixed fruit, sugar and butter
in a saucepan and heat gently until the butter has melted and
the sugar has dissolved. Stir the mixture and let it cook for
3–4 minutes more, until the fruit has plumped up a little
and is shiny and glistening. Set aside.
　Preheat the oven to 190°C/375°F/gas mark 5. To make
the crumble, rub the butter into the flour until the mixture
resembles coarse breadcrumbs. Stir in the sugar and three-
quarters of the almonds.
　Spoon half of the crumble over the base of the tin and
lightly press down. Cover with the fruit. Scatter the
remaining crumble over the fruit and then sprinkle with the
remaining flaked almonds. Bake for 30 minutes, until golden.
　Leave until completely cold and then cut into slices and
store in an airtight container.

Fennel Seed Cake

Makes 15
Preparation time: 1 hour
You will need a lightly buttered deep roasting pan
or rectangular cake tin measuring 20 x 30 cm/
8 x 12 inches

250 g/9 oz butter
250 g/9 oz caster sugar, plus extra to decorate
4 eggs, beaten
250 g/9 oz self-raising flour
2 teaspoons dried fennel seeds

The idea of adding fennel seeds to a sweet cake may
at first seem a little odd – but it tastes fabulous. Just
two teaspoons of fennel seeds will add the most
delicious hint of aniseed.

Preheat the oven to 180°C/350°F/gas mark 4. Cream the
butter and sugar together until light and fluffy and then add
the eggs, a little at a time until they are all fully incorporated.
Fold in the flour.
　Stir in the fennel seeds. Spoon the mixture into the
prepared tin and bake for about 30 minutes, or until golden
and springy.
　Leave to cool in the tin and then dust with caster sugar
and cut into squares. Store in an airtight tin,

Ginger Millionaire's Shortbread

Makes 16
Preparation time: 1 hour, plus setting time for the
toffee and chocolate
You will need a Swiss roll tin measuring
23 x 30 cm/9 x 12 inches

Shortbread
200 g/7 oz butter
200 g/7 oz plain flour
100 g/3½ oz ground rice
100 g/3½ oz sugar

Toffee layer
800 ml/1¼ pints condensed milk
200 g/7 oz butter
200 g/7 oz sugar
6 nuggets of crystallized ginger, roughly chopped

600 g/1 lb 5 oz dark chocolate

I have given this classic recipe a contemporary twist
by adding a little crystallized ginger – a slightly spicy
flavour that works very well paired with chocolate.

Preheat the oven to 180°C/350°F/gas mark 4. To make
the shortbread, rub the butter, flour, ground rice and sugar
together until the mixture forms a ball. Roll the shortbread
out to fit the tin and bake for 20 minutes, until golden and
firm to the touch. Remove from the oven and set aside.

To make the toffee layer, pour the condensed milk into
a heavy-based saucepan and add the butter and sugar.
Stir over a medium heat until the butter has melted and
the sugar is dissolved, and then turn down the heat and
bubble for 10 minutes, or until the mixture is thick,
golden and fudge-like. Stir in the ginger and spread over
the shortbread base. Leave until the toffee is completely
cold and set.

Melt the chocolate in a bowl over a saucepan of gently
simmering water. (Alternatively microwave on high for
1 minute.) Spread the chocolate over the toffee layer and
leave until it has set.

Cut the shortbread into bars and store in an airtight
container in a cool place.

Golden Syrup Cakes

Makes 15
Preparation time: 1 hour and 10 minutes
You will need a lightly buttered deep roasting tin
or cake tin measuring 20 x 30 cm/8 x 12 inches

300 g/10 oz golden syrup
300 ml/10 fl oz soured cream
150 g/5 oz caster sugar
3 eggs, beaten
250 g/9 oz butter, melted
300 g/10 oz plain flour
2 teaspoons baking powder

Preheat the oven to 180°C/350°F/gas mark 4. Beat the
golden syrup, soured cream, sugar and eggs together until
smooth. Whisk in the melted butter.

Sift the flour and baking powder together and add to the
cake mixture, stirring well to remove any lumps. Pour the
mixture into the prepared tin and bake for 45–50 minutes,
or until golden and springy.

Leave the cake to cool in the tin and then cut into squares.
Store in an airtight container.

Streusel Topped Blueberry Cake

Makes 15
Preparation time: 1 hour and 10 minutes, plus
30 minutes resting
You will need a lightly buttered deep roasting tin
or cake tin measuring 20 x 30 cm/8 x 12 inches

250 g/9 oz butter
250 g/9 oz sugar
4 eggs, beaten
250 g/9 oz self-raising flour
300 g/10 oz blueberries

Streusel
100 g/3½ oz butter
150 g/5 oz plain flour
100 g/3½ oz light muscovado sugar
2 tablespoons walnuts, chopped

Preheat the oven to 180°C/350°F/gas mark 4. Cream the
butter and sugar together until light and fluffy and then add
the eggs, a little at a time until they are all fully incorporated.
Stir in the flour, and then carefully fold in the blueberries.
Spoon into the prepared tin.

To make the streusel, rub the butter into the flour and
sugar until the mixture resembles coarse breadcrumbs. Stir
in the walnuts. Spoon evenly over the cake batter in the
tin. Bake for 30 minutes or so, until golden and springy.

Leave to cool in the tin and then cut into squares or bars.
Store in an airtight container.

Cinnamon Spiced Apple and Cider Cake

Makes 15
Preparation time: 1 hour and 10 minutes, plus
30 minutes resting for pastry
You will need a lightly buttered deep roasting tin
or cake tin measuring 20 x 30 cm/8 x 12 inches

250 g/9 oz butter
250 g/9 oz caster sugar, plus extra for sprinkling
4 eggs, beaten
250 g/9 oz self-raising flour
2 teaspoons ground cinnamon
3 apples, cored and diced
50 ml/2 fl oz cider

Preheat the oven to 180°C/350°F/gas mark 4. Cream the
butter and sugar together until light and fluffy and then add
the eggs, a little at a time until they are all fully incorporated.
Sift together the flour and the cinnamon and stir into the
cake mixture. Add the apples and cider and stir until
thoroughly combined. Spoon into the prepared tin and
bake for 30 minutes or so, until golden and springy.

   Leave to cool in the tin and cut into squares. Store in
an airtight container.

Cherry Speckled Lemon and Almond Bars

Makes 15
Preparation time: 1 hour and 10 minutes
You will need a lightly buttered, deep roasting pan
or cake tin measuring 20 x 30 cm/8 x 12 inches

250 g/9 oz butter
500 g/1 lb 2 oz sugar
4 eggs
200 g/9 oz self-raising flour
200 g/9 oz ground almonds
150 g/5 oz dried cherries
juice and zest of 1 lemon
1 tablespoon caster sugar, for sprinkling

Preheat the oven to 180°C/350°F/gas mark 4. Cream the
butter and sugar together until light and fluffy. Add the eggs,
a little at a time, stirring in between each addition, until the
mixture is smooth and all the eggs are incorporated.

   Stir in the flour and the ground almonds, and then add
the dried cherries, lemon zest and lemon juice, mixing well.
Spoon the mixture into the prepared tin and bake for
40–45 minutes until golden and firm to the touch.

   Remove from the oven and allow to cool in the tin,
sprinkle with caster sugar and then cut into bars. Store in
an airtight container.

Saffron and Buttermilk Squares with Honey Butter Glaze

Makes 15
Preparation time: 1 hour
You will need a lightly buttered deep roasting pan
or rectangular cake tin measuring 20 x 30 cm/
8 x 12 inches

Cake
pinch saffron
300 g/11 oz caster sugar
50 g/1¾ oz butter
3 eggs
225 ml/8 fl oz buttermilk
175 g/6 oz self-raising flour

Glaze
100 g/3½ oz butter
2 tablespoons runny honey

The saffron in these little cakes gives them a beautiful deep golden-orange colour with little wispy strands of red here and there, while the glaze adds a sweet, buttery gloss. Choose a light, flowery honey to make sure that you don't mask the delicate flavour of the saffron. Although saffron can be expensive, a little goes a long way. Make sure that you use saffron strands rather than ground saffron, however, as you will get much better results.

Preheat the oven to 180°C/350°F/gas mark 4. Put the saffron strands into a small bowl and cover with two tablespoons of just-boiled water. Leave to stand for at least 30 minutes – a couple of hours is possible.

Beat the sugar and butter together until light and fluffy and then slowly add the eggs, a little at a time, until they are fully incorporated.

Stir in the buttermilk and then the flour. Beat thoroughly until very smooth and then finally, stir in the saffron and its soaking liquid.

Spoon the mixture into the prepared tin and bake for 30 minutes, or until golden and springy.

Meanwhile, gently melt the butter and honey for the glaze together in a pan set over a low heat. Remove the cake from the oven and leave it to cool for two or three minutes, then spoon the glaze evenly over the cake.

Leave the cake to cool in the tin before cutting it into squares. Store in an airtight container.

Fresh Fig Cake

Makes 15
Preparation time: 1 hour
You will need a lightly buttered deep roasting pan
or rectangular cake tin measuring 20 x 30 cm/
8 x 12 inches

250 g/9 oz butter
250 g/9 oz caster sugar, plus extra to decorate
4 eggs, beaten
250 g/9 oz self-raising flour
100 g/3½ oz ground almonds
6 fresh figs

Perfect for a fall picnic, the fresh flavours of this
mouthwatering cake celebrate the season.

Preheat the oven to 180°C/350°F/gas mark 4. Cream the
butter and sugar together until light and fluffy and then add
the eggs, a little at a time until they are all fully incorporated.
Fold in the flour and the ground almonds.

   Cut the figs into large dice and carefully fold them into
the cake mixture. Spoon the mixture into the prepared tin
and bake for about 40 minutes, or until golden and springy.

   Leave to cool in the tin and then dust with caster sugar
and cut into squares. Store in an airtight container.

Strawberry Macaroon Bars

Makes 15
Preparation time: 1hour, plus 30 minutes resting
for the pastry
You will need a Swiss roll pan measuring
20 x 30 cm/8 x 12 inches

Pastry
175 g/6 oz butter
50 g/1¾ oz caster sugar
1 egg yolk
320 g/11 oz plain flour, sieved
450 g/1 lb strawberry jam

Topping
6 egg whites
175 g/6 oz caster sugar
85 g/3 oz ground almonds
2 tablespoons ground rice

Cream the butter and sugar together until light and smooth
and then beat in the egg yolk. Add the flour, and bring the
mixture together to form a smooth dough. Wrap the pastry
in plastic wrap and chill in the fridge for 30 minutes.

   Set the oven to 180°C/350°F/gas mark 4. Roll the pastry
out to cover the base of the tray and trim the edges neatly.
Spread the jam evenly over the pastry.

   In a clean bowl, whisk the egg whites and half the sugar
together until they form stiff peaks. Fold in the remaining
sugar. Carefully fold in the ground almonds and the ground
rice. Spread the mixture evenly over the jam.

   Bake for 25–30 minutes, until golden and firm. Allow the
cake to cool in the tin and then cut it into slices. Store in an
airtight container.

Iced Coconut Squares

Makes 15
Preparation time: 1 hour, plus cooling
You will need a lightly buttered, deep roasting tin
or cake tin measuring 20 x 30 cm/8 x 12 inches

250 g/9 oz butter
250 g/9 oz caster sugar
4 eggs, beaten
250 g/9 oz self-raising flour

Icing
400 g/14 oz icing sugar
100 g/3½ oz desiccated coconut

Preheat the oven to 180°C/350°F/gas mark 4. Cream the
butter and sugar together until pale and fluffy and then beat
in the eggs, a little at a time until the mixture is smooth.
You may have to add a little flour in between each addition
to prevent the mixture from curdling. When the eggs are
fully incorporated, add the remaining flour. Spoon into the
prepared tin and bake for 40 minutes or so, until risen and
golden. Cool in the tin.

To make the icing mix the icing sugar with enough water
to make a consistency similar to thick pouring cream. Pour
over the cake, scatter over the coconut and leave to set. Cut
into squares and store in an airtight container.

Rum and Raisin Brownies

Makes 15
Preparation time: 1 hour, plus 30 minutes soaking
You will need a lightly buttered roasting tin or cake
tin measuring 20 x 30 cm/8 x 12 inches

50 g/1¾ oz raisins
3 tbsp rum
250 g/9 oz butter
500 g/1 lb 2oz caster sugar
100 g/3½ oz cocoa powder
4 eggs, beaten
100 g/3½ oz self-raising flour
100 g/3½ oz walnuts, roughly chopped

Pour the rum over the raisins and set them aside to soak for
30 minutes.

Preheat the oven to 180°C/350°F/gas mark 4. Melt the
butter, sugar and cocoa powder together. Remove from the
heat and leave to cool slightly.

Stir the eggs into the cocoa mixture and fold in the flour.
Stir in the raisins and soaking liquid, together with the
walnuts. Spoon the mixture into the prepared tin and bake
for 35 minutes, or until just firm but still slightly fudgy.

Leave to cool in the tin and then cut into squares. Store
in an airtight container.

Index

M

Mango and Pistachio Bars 26

N

No Nut Brownies
Nuts:
  Almond and Chocolate Fudge Squares 78
  Almond Slices 25
  Banana and Pecan Squares 66
  Blueberry and Hazelnut Bars 66
  Cherry Speckled Lemon and Almond Bars 88
  Chocolate and Chestnut Bars 80
  Chocolate, Pear and Macadamia Nut Brownies 37
  Cranberry, Apple and Almond Squares 54
  Date and Walnut Squares 10
  Iced Cherry and Almond Squares 17
  Lemon and Almond Bars 30
  Mango and Pistachio Bars 26
  Pine Nut and Almond Bars 41
  Pistachio and Almond Bars 20
  Prune, Armagnac and Almond Brownies 44
  Sticky Pecan Slices 41
  Toffee and Hazelnut Shortbread Crumble Bars 27
  White Chocolate and Almond Brownies 74

O

Orange Blossom Honey and Sesame Bars 49
Orange Marmalade and Chestnut Brownies 68

P

Pear and Polenta Slices 67
Pine Nut and Almond Bars 41
Pistachio and Almond Bars 20
Plum Cakes 57
Plum Frangipane Slices 14
Prune, Armagnac and Almond Brownies 44
Prune Breton Bars 31

R

Raspberry and Mascarpone Shortbread 60
Raspberry and White Chocolate Squares 54
Ricotta Slices 16
Rosemary and Raisin Squares 13
Rum and Raisin Brownies 93

S

Saffron and Buttermilk Squares with
  Honey Butter Glaze 90
Spices:
  Apple and Cinnamon Slices 62
  Banana and Nutmeg Custard Brownies 38
  Caribbean Rum and Spice Bars 78
  Iced Crystallized Ginger Squares 77
  Rosemary and Raisin Squares 13
  Spiced Gingerbread Bars 30
  Spiced Pear Slices 62
  Spiced Pumpkin Squares 68
Spiced Gingerbread Bars 30
Spiced Pear Slices 62
Spiced Pumpkin Squares 68
Strawberry Macaroon Bars 91
Sticky Coconut and Chocolate Bars 48
Sticky Fruit and Whisky Slice 47
Sticky Pecan Slices 41
Streusel Topped Blueberry Cake 87
Sticky Toffee Squares 40

T

Toffee and Hazelnut Shortbread Crumble Bars 27
Treacle Slices 40

W

Walnut Squares, Date and 10
White Chocolate and Almond Brownies 74

Z

Zesty Apricot and Pecan Squares 48

First published in 2005 by Conran Octopus Limited,
a part of Octopus Publishing Group,
2–4 Heron Quays, London E14 4JP
www.conran-octopus.co.uk

Publishing Director: Lorraine Dickey
Commissioning Editor: Katey Day
Art Direction: Chi Lam and Carl Hodson
Designer: Victoria Burley
Production Manager: Angela Couchman
Photography: Tara Fisher
Prop Stylist: Róisín Neild
Home Economy: Liz Franklin

British Cataloguing-in-Publication Data.
A catalogue record for this book is available from the
British Library.

ISBN 1 84091 415 7

To order please ring Conran Octopus Direct
on 01903 828503.

Printed and bound in China

Author's Acknowledgments

With huge thanks to the brilliant team at Conran Octopus,
in particular Katey Day, my editor – for asking me to
write this book first of all and being so great to work with
throughout. To Chi Lam, Victoria Burley and Carl Hodson
for creating a book that looks every bit as delicious as the
recipes inside it. To Tara Fisher, for stunning photography –
and being so fab to work with at the shoot. Lastly but by
no means least, to all my friends for testing and tasting the
recipes, and to my wonderful sons, Chris, Tim and Oliver,
who munched their way happily through every page.